Almost 365

EMPOWERING Stories

Stories & Poems that will inspire and empower you,
and bring more laughter, joy and love to your life!

Almost 365 Empowering Stories

Layout Design and Print by: PrintingLegacy.com

ISBN: 9781693337604

Printed in Canada

ACKNOWLEDGEMENTS

The 365 Empowering Stories supports all in their quest to better themselves and others. This series shares stories that are motivating, inspiring, about lessons learned and poems. They give us the motivation to lead a happy, healthy and wealthy life.

There is a personal struggle in writing, whether the difficulty is getting the words to paper, sharing something they have never told before, healing themselves, or not being sure what to share. The journey the authors go on is not easily done.

I am grateful for all the authors who have chosen to make a difference in the world by sharing their own experiences in the hopes that the reader will get something from it, a nugget, that will help them through their own life's challenges.

Firstly, I would like to thank all the incredible authors that have contributed to this book and being patient as we work through completing all the stories. Your stories have made such an incredible impact on individuals all over the world. You are changing lives!!!

I would like to thank Linsey Fischer for her contribution to editing the book.

I leave this legacy for my children. Joey, Benny, Daniel, and David are beautiful young men; they are the love and light of my life. As they grow and find themselves in this huge world we live in, I am flabbergasted at how they think, the actions they take and the direction they are headed. I love you more than you will ever know. xo

I want to thank my brother Richard Goodman and sister Staci Goodman for always being there to talk to. I cherish my relationship with both of you more than you know. My gorgeous and brilliant nieces, Brooke and Cori, you are turning into such beautiful young ladies, I am so proud of your growth as giving and loving human beings. I love you all with all of my heart.

I miss all four of my grandparents who are no longer here. They are always with me in my heart and in my mind; I miss them dearly. You were my best friends, my solace when I needed to get away, a friend when I needed to talk, I really miss you all and think of you all the time; Kate and Joseph Goodman (Grumpy), Sala and Ber Blady (Grumpy).

Thank you to my mom, Mary Goodman, who would always be there if you needed someone. It was a transition year for you, and I only wish you to be healthy and happy. You have had your own struggles throughout and have taught me to be compassionate and caring above all else.

Thank you to my D.O.D. (Dear Old Dad), Phil Goodman, for always being there for me, regardless of my age, and for treating me with respect, even if you didn't like the conversation. I love and appreciate both of my parents.

Thank you, Linda and Zach, my younger brother (30 years younger), for always being a smiling face and open to chat with. I love you both.

To our volunteers and partners who tirelessly work to make everything a success, I am grateful for you and can't thank you enough.

I want to thank my friends who love giving back and helping others! Surround yourself by those you look up to.

~Randi Goodman

Table of Contents

Introduction

Linsey Fischer

Books excel at bringing people together in a unique way. The readers have the opportunity to connect with the author as fellow authors get to experience sharing their stories as one.

This collection of empowering stories reminds us that no matter what walk of life you come from, you have the ability to uplift yourself and others. Through taking a chance, and allowing yourself to open up your heart to the world, you allow yourself to step out of the shadows and into the spotlight to share your message.

Once you embrace the pages of this book, you will go inside the minds of the writers as they convey their most vulnerable life experiences with you. The reader can allow themselves to escape into the lives of the writer, where similarities can be found as you compare your own life experiences or those of a friend or family member. You may laugh, cry, smile, but most importantly, learn something new as new insights begin resonate with you.

Even if you can't relate to every chapter, you can always take away a message of hope, love, strength, support, and guidance. May each person who opens this book, gain the courage to share their own story with others one day.

Just be you!

by Randi Goodman

Be real in every relationship in your life, don't be a phony to others, and especially not to yourself. Oh, excuse my words, did I actually say that? How does that help you anyway?

To live a happy and fulfilled life you need to remove toxic people from it and sometimes that means family, friends or business associates. If you can't remove family (because the person is a parent, sibling or child), then limit your time with them so they don't affect your headspace or actions. I have experienced this and it is no fun; all you want to do is have a great relationship with them, but it just doesn't work the way you desire.

Being authentic and vulnerable in business will draw people to you, but when you hold back, you can appear cold and unapproachable. Being genuine in your personal life sometimes scares people off, but who is it that you want to attract? Do you want to attract people who love you for who you are or do you want to attract people who want you to be fake and lie to them?

A family member once told me that they were always afraid of me growing up because they never knew what would come out of my mouth. Once we were in our thirties, that person told me they loved and appreciated who I was because they knew they were always getting the real person. That doesn't mean you should speak your mind and offend people, but it does mean you shouldn't lie to them. When people know you are truthful or authentic and live with integrity, they learn to love you, trust you—and in business, buy from you!

Let's make the world a better place by living lives of honesty, integrity and love!

Randi Goodman has four beautiful boys (young men), and is a 4th level CMA; a 6x #1 International Best-Selling Author; a Licensed Real Estate Sales Person; a 2nd Degree Black Belt; and an International Speaker. She has devoted years to producing Charity Gala's and has run a manufacturing company, which prompted her to create business-to-business events to help entrepreneurs. Randi has produced almost 60 #1 International best-selling authors with her international book series, *Empowering Women to Succeed;* and has over 145,000 students with her online courses in over 170 countries. She has showcased hundreds of experts on her podcast and on stage at her live events, where she has also promoted 100s of exhibitors and coaches corner experts and connected 1000s of entrepreneurs.

Websites:
www.torontowomensexpo.com
www.empoweringwomentosucceed.com
www.randigoodman.ca
www.randigoodmanrealestate.com
Podcast: https://empowermentradioshow.com
Twitter: @RandiConnects | @TOWomensExpo
Facebook: Toronto Women's Expo | Randi Goodman Real Estate
LinkedIn: /randingoodman/
Instagram: @randig71

If I Can Do It, What About You?

by Agnola Charles-Snowball

At age sixty-four, turning one of my poems into a children's book, "What Happens to Numbers 1 to 10?" was one of the most amazing things I have ever done, and I am extremely proud that I did it.

I reached out for help from friends and family, but got more negative responses than positive ones. I even got turned down by one publisher. However, I pressed on and did not give up. I showed my work to my husband David and my friend Pam, who helped with the editing. Another friend, Lynn from church helped with the coordination of it. I am extremely grateful that I had the help and encouragement from these three people in my life.

On my journey to getting my book published, I had to learn how to be an artist too. I went on the internet and taught myself how to draw a zoo and different types of animals. I even amazed myself by drawing pictures of boys and girls, trees, flowers, the earth, and the sky. You name it, and I did it. I learned by making considerable amounts of mistakes. But, in the process, I never gave up on my dreams of becoming a first-time author. I realized in those moments that I could do anything I put my mind to.

One of the major reasons I wrote this book was to make learning fun for all children. Another reason was to inspire them. The final reason I wrote this book was to show children and even adults that they are never too old or too young to accomplish their goals. If I can write my first book at age sixty-four, nothing is impossible for them to do. I have been getting much positive feedback from families about how well children are responding to this book, and it makes me feel that I have accomplished my goal of reaching them.

If I can do it, what about you?

Agnola Charles-Snowball was born in Antigua. She lives in Toronto, Canada and has two daughters and four grandchildren. She graduated from George Brown College in 1996 as a medical administrator, and currently works as a physician's administrator. Agnola has written many inspirational songs and poems, and her first children's book.

http://www.agnolacharles.com/

Your Inner Voice Has a Purpose

by Alie Amaral

The memory of March 8, 2004, no longer hurts; however, I vividly recall the excruciating pain in my heart, and how I clutched it because it was all I understood. That was the day I decided to leave my marriage of over fifteen years, and the beginning of my estrangement.

Every step we take leaves an imprint. I spent the next three years in battle, in a kind of trance, as a result of my exodus. I left everything behind because I simply could no longer stay—my inner voice was screaming for release! And so began the fight within me, and externally. Both were fierce.

Despite the support of my family, I experienced the biggest and deepest feelings of loneliness, emptiness, and sadness. I wailed every night before bed in deep lamentation.

Nothing mattered to me except being with my daughters. All I was able to do for three years was observe them from a distance, and throughout this time, my family's encouragement always surrounded me. Sometimes I felt they feared I might consider returning to the marriage, but life presented me with the most surprising turns and what seemed initially to be a misfortune, later became a blessing.

It turned out that my inner voice had a purpose, and I listened to it. Deep in my heart, I knew that I was ready to move forward with my life as a single mom, so I kept reminding myself of who I was. It didn't matter that I didn't have it all figured out. I accepted that I was truly ready to start living my life.

What was going on? I followed my heart! Little did I know that the pain of my past would birth the gifts that my current business provides, taking people on a "journey to grace, faith, and self-love." It has been so rewarding. How did I do it? I had faith in the magical power of love and completely trusted in myself. I believed deeply that what I truly wanted would come to me!

 Alie Amaral lives in Oakville, Ontario, with her family. Her divorce forced her vulnerability. It was through this emotional state that she was transformed through the power of unconditional love, for self. She now supports her clients to open their hearts, so they too can discover who they really are.

Contact: alie@heartquestliving.com

Instagram: https://www.instagram.com/alie__amaral/

Facebook: https://www.facebook.com/almerinda.amaral

Website: https://www.heartquestliving.com/

LinkedIn: https://www.linkedin.com/in/alie-amaral-98916830

Blessings of Invisible Illness

by Alison Coombs

Interstitial cystitis? "What is that?" When you have an invisible illness that few have heard of, it makes you question your sanity. Was I crazy? Intense pain mixed with thoughts of ending my life. Crazy or not, I couldn't live like that forever. After all, I was only nineteen. If I couldn't be well, I didn't want to live.

Luckily, hope had different plans for me. It came in the form of a book. Before I was correctly diagnosed, I saw many specialists, was misdiagnosed many times and was given lots of unnecessary treatments. Nothing worked! Not one thing. After reaching a really low point, I went online and searched for anything that could help me get better. That is where I found my hope. There was a book about a woman with a severe case of Interstitial cystitis who was now living in remission.

I was so excited. I ordered the book from Amazon and read her story in one sitting. This newfound hope helped me choose to be persistent with getting well not only physically, but emotionally and spiritually too. Hope and the decision to take my health into my own hands is what saved my life. It wasn't easy, but guess what? I got better! I used a few of the book's suggestions, additional online resources, and I visited two holistic practitioners. I slowly made healthy lifestyle changes and became the best version of myself possible. The combination of these things sent my illness into remission.

Do I have occasional flares? Yes. Do I remain in a defeated place? No. I now choose to find the silver lining in every situation and to be persistent regarding the things I can control in my life. This illness is a blessing in disguise as it helped me choose to live a healthy lifestyle and help others to do the same. Through my wellness business, I help women choose health so they can avoid the pain I felt. All of our daily actions either help us improve our health or rob us of it, so choose health every day.

Alison Coombs is a mother, wife, and fitness professional who is passionate about holistic health and creating an army of fit moms. She's dedicated to helping moms strengthen their bodies, manage their weight, and increase their energy levels. Her services include in-home personal training, wellness coaching, and virtual boot camps.

Website: www.alisoncoombs.com

Instagram: www.instagram.com/alisonvcoombs

Facebook: https://www.facebook.com/alisonvcoombs/

Inexpensive Taste

by Aliya Singh

Your image does not have to depend on what the latest fashion magazines are throwing at you— personal style is much more unique than that!

I grew up with the concept that fashion does not have to cost a fortune. When we were children, our family would invest in the home, vacations, and experiences, never in expensive clothes. Yet, all three of us children always looked polished and well put together. At a very young age, I learned that it was the pieces, not the prices that distinguished a polished look. My mother dressed up as elegant as can be. Every detail was so well put together that she always looked so polished.

Like many young daughters, I'd love to play dress up. I'd often shimmy around in her heels, put on her cloche hats, and wrap her necklaces around me as I'd pretend to walk a runway feeling like a million bucks. What I'd later learn and appreciate is the fact that all her items were never designer, overly expensive, or one of a kinds; they were just reasonably priced, basic retail store pieces (some even vintage or second hand) that were just put together so beautifully with style, grace, and great taste! Learning this at a young age, I quickly caught on that creativity with price tags and pieces is key.

This is what inspired me to start my image consulting business. Studying the science of style, I never bought into the idea that garments would have to be overly expensive to be classic. Instead, my goal was to empower women to translate their personality, taste, and most importantly, unique style to create their look. Personal image is not about fashion per se; it's a way to express your unique vision of style and express yourself—no matter what your size, age, or budget! These lessons and tools I learned from at such a young age—only now am I able to fully appreciate and use my experience to help empower *all* women through their personal style.

Aliya Singh studied fashion management and image consulting to gain extensive knowledge in the industry. She has worked with leaders including Jubilee Jewelers, MAC Cosmetics, FASHION magazine, Slice Network, and Hair Club in management, sales, and marketing. Aliya launched True You in 2010 to transform her passions into a business!

www.trueyou.ca

You Deserve Happiness and Freedom

by Amanda McNair

Imagine a life where you love yourself completely, you're with the partner of your dreams, your career lights you up, you have an abundance of money, you vacation as often as you want, and you're truly happy with your life.

How would you spend your ideal day?

How would you feel?

How can you make this happen for yourself?

No really; take a moment and reflect on those questions before reading any further. Most people get to that third question and assume they can't make it happen, but they're missing out on a huge piece of the puzzle: we're all in control of our lives.

It may not always feel that way; maybe you believe you've been dealt some less than desirable circumstances, but it's not about the situations you face—it's about what you make them mean. What you think about your circumstances is what causes your feelings, and it's those feelings that lead to the actions you take (or inactions you don't take) that create your life experience.

Think that's a load of crap? Okay, continue living the current life you're not thrilled about.

Or, take a chance; choose to elevate your mindset and become self-aware. Aware of the thoughts you have, the feelings they cause, and the actions you take—that either create a positive or negative life experience for you. You can choose to tune in to your own intuition; to do what feels most authentic to you.

Wouldn't it be liberating to speak your truth, instead of saying what you think other people want to hear?

Wouldn't it be empowering to take action for yourself, instead of doing what everyone else asks you to do?

Wouldn't it be exciting to turn your dreams into your reality, instead of doing what's expected of you?

You have the power to make this happen. I know because I did it. And I'm never looking back. We all deserve to have the life we actually want for ourselves, a life of happiness and freedom.

Amanda McNair uses unleashed and uncensored coaching techniques to help you develop a strong mindset, build fierce confidence, and create your best life. Her uniquely intuitive coaching and passion for self-empowerment will guide you to overcome your excuses—and choose to take control of how you experience your life.

https://www.authenticsoulcoaching.com/

https://www.facebook.com/Authentic.Soul.Coaching

https://www.instagram.com/authentic.soul.coaching/

What I Would Tell My Twenty-Year-Old Self

by Andrea Stapley

Don't work so hard and enjoy life. When you start moving away from your happy, free-spirited self, re-group, pay attention to those changes, and take care of yourself so you can get back to being you!

Face the world fearlessly; everything that's worth it sits on the other side of fear.

Spend every penny you make on travel while you are young with less responsibilities. See the world while you can and make a contribution to it.

Find something you love that nourishes your soul. Don't prioritize other things over that.

Support the family, friends, and young women you can coach and mentor to build them up and teach them how amazing and strong they are.

All those good ideas that are risky? Do them. You will regret not starting that business or buying that investment property even though you can't afford it.

Stay home with your babies. They are only little once. Soak up every minute because as a powerhouse woman you can pick up where you left off in your career. Don't let fear hold you back.

Worry less about your weight and what you look like. It's a prison sentence and sucks the joy out of your life. Focus on being healthy and taking care of you because you're beautiful and perfect the way you are.

Find someone who loves you for the amazing woman you are. If they don't contribute to making you want to be a better person they are probably not the one!

Spend your life making a difference in people's lives. Let your purpose be that you impacted many and helped them to have a better life because you existed. Don't make your life all about you and your tiny circle.

Make family and friends the priority always; don't waste precious time with acquaintances. Tell your family every day you love them and forgive always.

Be you. Everyone can smell your bull from a mile away even when you think you're hiding it and pretending life is perfect.

Love fiercely and live a life you love.

Andrea Stapley, BA, is the assistant vice president of cloud computing at Sun Life Financial and has worked in information technology for twenty-six years.

She is a #1 international best-selling author of "Empowering Women to Succeed—Leap," and is most passionate about being a wife and mother of two.

Finding Your Passion and Resilience to Thrive

by Andrea Watson

So where does one's passion and resilience really come from? These attributes are often used as buzz words and credited as the foundation of many successes. I wanted to understand them and dive into my own journey as I hope to inspire others to uncover and embrace their own magical powers.

I have found that passion and resilience are not things you can pinpoint. Passion evolves and exudes from your inner desires to give the best of yourself. How do you mold and create resilience? Not from a title, nor any amount of experience, a mix of good or bad, or even the people who shaped you. It's a whole smorgasbord! And yes, that goes back to where we all began to know ourselves. What drove us to try new things? How did we get back up when we fell? Who and what inspired us along the way?

With the joys of motherhood, I felt a deep responsibility to guide my daughter. It was during the trauma of single parenthood when she was under two, that my full-circle moment unfolded. My history flooded back, and I recalled how it all began for me.

Born to teenage parents, my siblings and I faced their addictions; mental health; neglect; physical and emotional abuse; and our low-income conditions. When I share my experiences, I am often asked how did I make it through? The only answer I find each time is I chose to stay positive. Being the protective big sister and mini mommy since age five, I had to step up. I also found great friends who helped encourage my full potential.

Over a year ago, I helped launch Nature Knows Inc. Though a major risk, I left the safety of a big corporate job to make a much bigger impact! I called upon my array of skills and deep-rooted resilience. Tough changes were kind of "normal" for me. I have always been outgoing and passionate to give back. It's now my purpose, helping to nourish the world! We can all choose our path and make a difference. I hope you will find yours!

Andrea Watson is a proud mother, entrepreneur, and volunteer. Passionate about giving back, she loves food, wine, travel, and quality time with family and friends. Beginning her career in fashion, she moved to foodservice with leading CPG companies working in sales and marketing and is now CEO, Nature Knows Inc.

www.natureknows.ca

In Pursuit of a Better Life

by Anna Vujovic

When I look back at my early life, surrounded by loving family and friends in Sarajevo, I see happiness, contentment, and a mapped-out future. In 1991, I started university and had loving parents, a younger sister, and my first serious boyfriend. But, the downfall of a mapped-out future is almost complete helplessness once it is taken away from you. On April 6, 1992, my country woke up to find that the embers of civil war had become a full-blown fire. My only hope was to leave without looking back.

I escaped overnight and arrived in Slovenia, where I was in the country illegally and didn't speak the language. The war was raging at home, I had no way of going back, and my family had no way of reaching me. I couldn't go back to school. For two years, I floated between random jobs I could get as a refugee. My only goal was to find a place far away and the opportunity for a better life. I chose Canada.

The initial period of adjustment was hard: a new language, a new way of life, new friends. But I would always see that pot of gold at the end of the rainbow, my chance at the life I imagined as a nineteen-year-old back in Sarajevo. I worked, I studied, I made wonderful friends, I made my own family, and I reunited with my parents and sister. Following that rainbow, I arrived at the pinnacle of my life.

Today, I am the proud mother of a fifteen-year-old man who inspires me to be a better person every day. I found my career in real estate, and for the past fourteen years, I've been lucky to go to work every day with a joyful bounce in my step. I discovered one truth—passion and perseverance are key. If you are passionate about your life and goals that will give you the strength to succeed regardless of your circumstances, you can always start from the ground up. And you will go only up if you firmly believe that's the only way to go.

Anna Vujovic immigrated to Canada in 1994 as a government-sponsored refugee from the former Yugoslavia. Today, she is a successful global real estate advisor based in Toronto. She is also a single mother to a fifteen-year-old son and is active in support of children's charities.

www.annavujovic.ca

It Was Never Going to Happen to Me ... Until It Did.

by Anthony Rodrigo

It was never going to be me ... until it was. Thank goodness for second chances.

In August 2011, I made an unusual trip to Newmarket. My wife Angela and I kind of laugh about it now, but the truth is my unplanned visit was by ambulance to Southlake Hospital. My routine annual medical check-up (eighteen days prior) hadn't detected the 99 percent and 70 percent blockages in my left anterior descending artery (LAD).

At forty-three, I encountered a near-death experience—a sudden and unexpected heart attack—and learned that there are no coincidences in life; everything happens for a reason.

The hospital experience was a complete nightmare; I honestly felt that I would not make it out. I was admitted in the early afternoon through the emergency entrance, assessed, and then quickly taken back behind the curtain to where people in serious trouble wait. Angela stayed with me the entire time. We were both worried but didn't say it to each other. This could be lights out I kept thinking. The emergency doctor arrived and broke the news: I had lost 25 percent of my heart function and would be staying for a few days. She looked worried. The next thirty-six hours were a haze as I was pumped with five or six different drugs and had several procedures.

Since then, the small things that used to bother me have lost their influence. On any given day, I am not sure what the future holds, but my plan is to embrace everything that life will let me be a part of while I hang tightly onto Angela, the love of my life.

As I live my second chance, I am forever grateful for my family (the Rs, Ks, Is, Ms, Ps, and Cs) and all the experiences I've encountered in my life journey. These days, I continue my work in healthcare speaking about the connection between mental health and the manifestation of physical diagnoses, and the integrating of natural medicines in health and recovery.

Anthony Rodrigo, continues his 20 year consultative - Integrative Natural medicine Healthcare fitness and HealthRecovery™ compensation and benefits practice. He's a survivor of a common illness diagnosis, and a recipient of the resulting benefit all Canadians can be approved for, and he helped create.

Email Rodrigo@Rodrigoinc.com

Website https//www.ihealtheinstitute.com

Angels to the Rescue

by Baljeet Soor

It took me a long time to realize that I could stand up for myself. People that want to control and manipulate you, don't like it when you do find the courage to actually speak up and do what's right for yourself. To them, it means they no longer have that power over you, and they feel defeated. However, it's not about who wins or loses; it's about finding a way out in order to be yourself on your own terms.

After I left my ex-husband, he moved to a basement apartment half an hour away. Every weekend for almost five months, my daughters and I had stayed with him, so the kids could spend time with their father.

In the midst of his anger one night, he began choking me while we spoke in the garage, and just as abruptly, he let me go; my first sign of an angel's protection. I was shaking as I came downstairs to my daughters. They could sense something was wrong. I feared what he might do next and didn't want to take the chance of finding out.

My first chance to escape arrived when he went to the washroom and closed the door. I got my daughters into their coats and with one child under each arm, ran up the stairs as quickly as I could. I remember being scared that the stairs would creak as they normally did when I went up, but they didn't make a single sound; my second sign of an angel's protection.

Running from house to house at 11:00 p.m. on a snowy winter's night, felt like a movie scene. The sixth house finally answered their door, and a lovely couple helped us in and gave us warm socks and tea before the police arrived— my third sign of an angel's protection that night.

In my heart, I know I was guided to do what I had to do to protect my family. I was Divinely protected. The surge of energy and courage that came over me was indescribable and perfect.

Baljeet Soor is passionate about helping people understand the broad spectrum of good health. She does this through the manual science of osteopathy. Baljeet considers herself a lifelong learner of many things including parenthood, self-evolution, spiritualism, and the connection between mind, body, and soul.

www.goodhealthosteopathy.ca

https://www.instagram.com/good_health_osteo/

https://www.facebook.com/goodhealthosteopathy/

A Poem for Survivors of Verbal Abuse

by Baljeet Soor

You say I'm ugly.
You say no one wants me.
You say I'll never amount to anything.
You say I can never do anything right.
You say I'm useless.
You say I shouldn't even try.
You say your life would be better without me.
You say I'm stupid.
You say I can't cook.
You say I have to stay home.
You say my thighs are too big.
You say I'm pathetic.
You say you should have left me.
You say no one will ever love me.
You say I'll screw it all up.
You say I can't think right.

I say I'm done with all the things you say.
I say I'm beautiful.
I say I'm loving and loveable.

I say I can do anything.
I say I am useful.
I say I will try.
I say life is amazing with me in it.
I say I'm smart.
I say I can cook.
I say I can go anywhere.
I say my body is beautiful.
I say I'm awesome.
I say I should have left you long ago.
I say someone loves me.
I say I will make good things happen.
I say I can think for myself.
I say I respect myself enough to leave you.

Baljeet Soor is passionate about helping people understand the broad spectrum of good health. She does this through the manual science of osteopathy. Baljeet considers herself a lifelong learner of many things including parenthood, self-evolution, spiritualism, and the connection between mind, body, and soul.

www.goodhealthosteopathy.ca

https://www.instagram.com/good_health_osteo/

https://www.facebook.com/goodhealthosteopathy/

Jess and The Plate

by Barbara Jasper

Our words are powerful; one simple sentence can cheer someone on to victory or destroy their confidence. We may intend to convey one message, but oftentimes another, quite different one, is heard.

Growing up in a volatile environment, I often heard derogatory messages that I assumed were a normal part of life (which I later learned were absolutely not). Once I had my own children, my parenting skills were developed from reading books and seeing other great moms and dads parent. I thought I was doing a pretty good job.

And then one day, I slipped.

While having a very spirited argument with my eldest daughter she said to me, "Mom, when you said what you did the way you did, I felt like a plate you just smashed on the ground; broken, and in a lot of pieces… a mess. And even though you said sorry, I'm still the plate that's broken, inside. How can you fix that? You can't." Clearly, I had hurt her terribly.

Those words stung, but I knew she was absolutely right! Nothing I could say could bring her (the plate) back to its unbroken state.

But... I had learned about the Japanese art of Kintsukuroi (also called kintsugi), which is repairing cracked pieces of pottery with gold. The thought is that when an item is damaged, instead of getting rid of it, you seam it back together with a gold and dust mixture so that—in its own way—it's even more beautiful than it was before it was broken. The end result is a stunning piece that's been repaired and is as strong, and more beautiful, than it was when it was whole.

I am proud to say that I have a Kintsukuroi relationship with my daughter. I have repaired the damage with words of gold which has, in turn, strengthened our relationship. It is a lesson that I've held close to my heart ever since, and a story that I share often.

I'm so grateful to have had the learning opportunity to be a better Mom.

 Barbara Jasper inspires and teaches women to earn a living, doing what inspires them. In 2007, seeing a need, she founded Canada's first Teen Empowerment Magazine. That success led to her becoming a certified success coach, professional speaker, and personal branding expert who now works with women of all ages.

Website: https://barbarajasper.com/

The Wilderness

by Belinda Paradise

It was 2001, and I had lost everything. I had been in my job for four years, and I was in the process of purchasing my first home. I was also raising four children on my own, and my children and I were close. I felt like things were going well until I went to the doctor and got some disturbing news. After running some tests, the doctor told me I would need surgery. I was thirty-nine years old, and in line for a promotion in my job.

I had to tell my manager the news. He wasn't happy, but he allowed me to work until my surgery. After surgery, I was on sick leave for two months. Then I got the news that if I returned to my demanding position, I would be jeopardizing my health. I knew I had to resign from a position that would potentially worsen my health, and that there was the possibility that I would probably have to start over. It had taken me several years to earn that position. Now, I had to live on what I had saved and collect unemployment.

I could no longer purchase my new starter home, and I was disappointed. I eventually had to move out because I could no longer afford the living expenses. I made the decision to leave and move in with family temporarily until I was able to get back on my feet. I was devastated, and I began to lose faith and hope.

One day, I drove to the park while the kids were at school, and I sat there wondering, why did this happen to me? As tears began to roll down my face, I looked up at the sky and heard these words: *the wilderness*. I never realized I had the gift of writing until I was faced with an actual wilderness! I grabbed a pen and tablet and began to write my first poem. My misfortune helped me find my passion and gift within.

Many people are experiencing pain in society today. Belinda Paradise's passion for writing is to uplift and inspire the reader. Her unique gift and talent, coupled with spirituality, gives her the ability to write from a deep place within. Inspirational poetry is another part of her writings.

Email: poeticmoments7@gmail.com

Lessons from Life Seasons

by Beulah Thomson

"For everything there is a season."
Ecclesiastes 3:1

The rhythms of nature show us the fluidity of life. Nothing stays the same! God and the universe teach us wisdom through the natural seasons of life. Nature transitions effortlessly through its seasons. Therefore, to have effortless increase and fulfillment, we must understand and align ourselves with nature's cycles.

No season is permanent; we transition from one to the other. How long we stay in one season is dependent on our ability to take control of our minds and harness their power to create opportunities and favourable environment for our advancement.

Fall (Season of Letting Go)

Falling leaves, bare trees, and colder days represent a time of crisis and painful experiences which we must go through to learn the lessons that will make us stronger and better. Betrayals and disappointments of life seem insurmountable but learning to let go as the trees willingly let go of their leaves is crucial for our personal growth.

Winter (Season of Introspection)

The winters of life propel us into "night seasons" where we embark on an inward journey of introspection. We find ourselves isolated and at a crossroads, faced with the decision of either giving in to despair or accepting life's challenges, learning the lessons it offers and growing as a result.

Spring (Season of Opportunities)

Spring is our springboard for greatness. A season for new beginnings! It presents opportunities for advancement. Here, we set goals, develop new skills, and pursue our dreams with a sense of purpose and direction.

Summer (Season of Reaping)

Accomplishment, success, and abundance are words to describe this season. We have accomplished our goals. Our hard work has paid off. We feel fulfilled. We are inspired to achieve more! In addition, this is the time to network with new people, make financial investments from the harvest we reaped, and plan for our future goals.

Every season brings with it important insights and lessons. Whatever season you're facing right now, remember it won't last forever, but you can utilize it for your personal growth!

Beulah Thomson, B Pharm, MPH, is a #1 international bestselling author, international speaker, and peak performance coach. As the facilitator for Quantum Leap Breakthrough Academy, Beulah has empowered numerous people. Her radical training programs offer maximum productivity, achievement, and building innovative brands that stand out as industry leaders.

Website: https://beulahthomson.com

Facebook: https://www.facebook.com/beulahthomson1

Arriving Ethically

by Bev Patel

I was a real estate agent for nine years and loved it, but some days I felt there was a void. What was it? I loved this business of showing people houses and essentially making them feel they bought the home of their dreams. I definitely made sufficient money doing it. So why did I feel so empty?

Many, including my spouse, told me that being ethical and a REALTOR® didn't go hand-in-hand. Was that the joy I was missing? Was I too ethical? So, I carried on assisting buyers and sellers, but the real joy came from me helping people, finding the home and then falling asleep knowing I did my job ethically.

One day I thought how wonderful it would be if I could marry my knowledge of real estate and ethics. Maybe in a strange way, I threw my innermost desire out to the Universe. Well, the Universe spoke back in the form of a job posting! One of the real estate boards in Ontario was looking for a professional development specialist, and I proceeded to apply.

The next thing I knew, I was preparing for an interview and subsequently a second one to show my presentation skills. That brings me to now—hired and training other agents to love what they do and be ethical. That's a wonderful feeling; no amount of commission can bring that kind of satisfaction. Who knows what my next calling will be, but this really doesn't feel like work, it feels like passion because I'm true to myself and my beliefs. I've arrived!

So, remember, the truth is out there, but the key is to listen and hear it.

Before Bev Patel obtained her current job at one of the largest real estate boards in Toronto as a professional development specialist, her last nine years were spent as a REALTOR®, "Putting the 'Real' in Real Estate." Bev's motto: Honesty is a path towards success!

On Mentorship:
A Gift That Keeps on Giving

by Catherine King Ward

Early in my career, I was a supervisor for services to the disabled in Central Ontario public libraries. I took great pride in providing solutions that ensured compliance, well-being, and accessibility for all. My aptitude for people and process didn't go unnoticed. One day, Rosemary, my executive director, approached me with an opportunity that changed the trajectory of my professional life. She offered me the role of human resources (HR) coordinator.

Rosemary's guidance made her the first of my many invaluable mentors.

My transition into HR was marked with struggle as I entered a male-dominated industry—oil and steel—during an era when HR was considered non-essential and costly. But I viewed each day as a new learning opportunity. My favourite and most rewarding mentorship experience came from my former boss, Charlie, who mentored me for eighteen years. Charlie included me in core decision-making opportunities with key business leaders and taught me about sales, operations, and finances. With his support, I became a valuable HR leader and contributor.

My participation in instrumental business activities showcased my skills to other department managers and senior executives. I learned their areas of expertise and made it my mission to ensure their units never faced people problems. I provided them with the best employees, collaborated with them on HR strategy, and together, we worked towards common goals.

I was challenged daily, but paramount to my success was Charlie's leadership and mentorship. He never failed to answer my questions. He openly shared his ideas, and I did everything in my power to drive HR in the direction of his vision for the company. Charlie played an integral role in my success, and I am forever grateful.

I've had the good fortune of wonderful mentorship over the years, which is why I mentor others. I coach new HR graduates and start-up businesses, guide businesses in compliance, and mentor people through their job search.

If I could offer one piece of advice, it would be to take opportunities, work hard, and give back to others.

This is dedicated to my mother Dorothy, Rosemary and Charlie. Thank you.

Catherine King Ward is an HR professional passionate about helping businesses make the most of their resources and talent. She believes in challenging employees at every level to grow—to reach—and to perform at the edge of their abilities, and to feel proud of what they have accomplished.

https://www.linkedin.com/in/catherinekingward/

www.yourhrspecialist.ca

The True "Good" Life

by Chantelle Simone

The recipe for a good life is this: go to school, get good grades, and get a good job.

That's what *they* say, but is it really?

The False Reality

I was encouraged to follow this recipe as my parents wanted the best for me. It started off well: I achieved a bachelor's degree in finance, then a master black belt in business process improvement. I got a great job, earned a six-figure income with a multibillion-dollar company, and developed my real estate portfolio, but something was still missing. I was unfulfilled.

That *good* life was supposed to bring me satisfaction. *I did what they said*, yet I was dreading the sound of my alarm, agonizing over traffic, and feeling like a number among the herd of professionals. Is this it? There had to be more. It was time to find it.

The Truth

Deep down, we're all searching for that *thing* that lights us up. It allows us to experience the freedom, joy, and happiness we desire. I realized that thing is called *purpose*!

I knew I had a purpose beyond the office walls and was determined to live it.

I knew God created us not for a dull life, but for a life so satisfying we could barely believe it.

I knew that if I could see it in my mind, it *was possible* before my eyes.

My truth saved my life and gave me permission to live!

The Victory

The search began: seminars, courses, trainings, coaching, retreats, and spiritual guides. I experienced them all!

I learned to say "no" to anything, anyone, and any opportunity that stopped me from living my truth. Walking away from my job, some "friends," a marriage, and a business to take a stand for myself wasn't easy, but it was worth it.

Six years, thousands of dollars, and four master certifications later, I gained the clarity and confidence to operate in *my* purpose!

Now I live an empowered life of freedom dedicated to helping others save those years of searching by guiding them directly to *their* truth and purpose. Isn't it time?

Chantelle Simone, a transformational educator, and neuro-linguistic programming master coach, helps you overcome, shift perspectives, and demystify your true identity to live a life on purpose. Her revolutionary online courses and memberships are filled with thought-provoking, mind-shifting information that reveals deep truths, elevating you to the next level of life.

Website: www.chantellesimone.com

Instagram: @Chantellesimonelive

Podcast: https://chantellesimone.podbean.com/

How It All Started

by Charmaine Wynter

When I first began interior designing, I had no idea that's what it was; I just knew I wanted my surroundings to look nice. I was the youngest of eight in a blended family. My father was a Jamaican-born cabinet maker turned Canadian construction worker; my mother, also a Jamaican immigrant, worked at a nearby Alberta university in maintenance.

I had a fairly typical upbringing that was common for the time—school; homework; chores and babysitting Monday through Friday; and church twice on Sunday. Saturday was the day I held dear. My folks slept in till nine o'clock in the morning, so I had that time free and spent it re- arranging my bedroom furniture. Each week I'd move everything around into a completely new configuration. I had no idea that my folks would lie in bed and upon hearing me moving the furniture yet again, place bets that this would be the week I'd repeat a layout.

I'm not sure if I ever did because when I turned twelve my parents divorced, and upon my father's departure I asked my mother if I could rearrange the living room furnishings. Her agreement opened up a new world for me, but my talent went unnoticed by my family members who dismissed it as, oh, that's just Charmaine. It wasn't until my mother (renowned for her cooking) invited the ladies from the church over that my skills were noticed and defined. I heard words of surprised acclamation and prophesies of interior designer stardom.

Obviously, the road between then and now was paved with highs and lows. My family members had never seen anyone successful working in the ambiguous field of design, so they encouraged me to become a secretary or a nurse. I had to find the money and the determination within myself to pursue my passion. I'd like to say I did but the truth is interior design is my second career. I wasted years believing my well-meaning family. So, my message is if you have a passion, go for it!

 Charmaine Wynter, multi-award-winning Jamaican Canadian; Texas-based interior designer; businesswoman; Living Well Show host and HGTV pioneer, is touted for her distinct, luxurious living signature look. As the founder of Charmaine Wynter Interiors and her bespoke furniture line, Charmaine keeps busy with her international commissions and turnkey interior design services.

The Turning Point

by Chieko El-Jisri

In 1997, I was going through a very difficult time in my life and searching for answers to my suffering. My co-worker introduced me to a life counselor who came from Japan. I was not interested in religion, but I needed some advice badly.

The counselor told me, "If you practice Buddha's thoughts at the Dojo (temple), then you can change your life." At the time, I had no knowledge of Buddhism, but I remembered the expression, "you can change your life." Those words gave me hope.

Then in 2000, I attended my Japanese spiritual leader's fire ceremony event in New York. After the ceremony, the leader gave us special meditation lessons. This was not part of the program, and I was excited by his sudden gift. I was sitting in front of him and receiving his guidance directly.

I studied, practicing Buddhism at the Dojo and at home. Then I noticed that when I was chanting the mantra, I felt different, and gradually, my awareness became deeper. Later my spiritual leader explained how powerful chanting the mantra is and encouraged us to continually practice.

I cannot remember the year I met my Reiki practitioner, but she told me, "You are already receiving Qi, and a pinkish-red flower is blossoming in your abdomen. You will soon open your eyes and see unusual things or light; you already opened your ears and heard sounds." During her Reiki practice on me, both my hands were buzzing like electric waves.

A year later, when the Dalai Lama visited Toronto, I went with my friends and my son to the Rogers Centre. When the Dalai Lama showed up on the stage, then sat on his special couch, I saw his beautiful, crystal-clear, and shining aura but my friends and my son did not.

My spiritual leader told us, "You don't have to believe what I say, but search yourself for the right answer." Now I practice forgiveness of others and myself. It took 19 years for me to freely understand how to change my life and release the suffering.

Chieko El-Jisri was born in Okinawa, Japan and immigrated to Canada with her husband in 1980. They have lived in Toronto with their family ever since. Chieko is passionate about helping others and started a second career at sixty-two after graduating from college as a community service and support worker.

My Breakthrough for Our Redemption

by Chris-Beth Cowie

Cries for a murdered cousin, a failed business venture, fourteen years of hair loss and a negative bank account sucked me into a whirlwind of chaos and depression. Feelings of being alone, stuck, and a failure plagued my mind as the hooks of fears, lies, and insecurities ripped through my core leaving me mentally broken and barren at twenty-eight years old.

"Our Redemption Song" came from me as a light in the middle of my despair and awoke my heart, helping me reclaim my vision and my freedom.

Our Redemption Song

You and I can break the chains of mental poverty
By stepping into reality
And thinking of things that could be
For there is greatness within you and me
We have been created for a divine purpose
So our passions can shine through us
To change this world for you and me
We're in this together you see
It's not just about me
Just me, is like a selfie

Boxed in, trapped in isolation
Leading to the mental insanity
Which is not good for humanity

Stop listening and believing fears, lies, and insecurities
Start thinking and believing in the positive possibilities
This will guarantee no hold of mental slavery

Always remember
We are loved by God Almighty
Loved, valued and important
Let's stand up with divine authority
Breaking free from all captivity
Becoming the light we're meant to be
Living and sharing our redemption song.

The message is simple: now I know I can break through the roadblocks or redirect my path to accomplish my dreams. I have strengthened my mind by accepting reality and focusing on my positive vision. I know that God is with me. The truth is that greatness lies within me and I have value to share. I am relentlessly pursuing dreams because I know that victory is mine. The challenges of life will come; either you will be crushed by the pressure or you will overcome. Are you ready to win?

Chris-Beth Cowie is the founder of Empowered for Excellence, an entrepreneurial leadership training and consulting company. She and her team are dedicated to empowering people to leverage their strengths and adding value to the community.

Website: www.empoweredforexcellence.com

Twitter: https://twitter.com/empowered4x

Twitter: https://twitter.com/chrisbethcowie

My Path to Freedom

by Christine Monfriese

Ok, who's gonna piss me off today? That's the first question I asked myself once I drove out of the bus parking lot.

You see, I worked as a city bus driver for ten-and-a-half years. It was a dream job for me in the beginning, because I love driving—especially big vehicles. Over the years, I worked every shift available: blue night (9:00 p.m. – 5:00 a.m.); late relief (6:00 p.m. – 2:00 a.m.); splits (6:00 a.m. – 9:00 a.m., and 2:00 p.m. – 6:00 p.m.); and early regulars (4:30 a.m. – 2:00 p.m.). I've transported and met thousands of people from all walks of life, but I've also endured a lot of verbal abuse. It became the norm; something you would expect at least once before week's end.

I've hustled a rum cake business on the side for many years. As I began to literally hate my full- time job due to overwhelming stress, I thought about my side hustle more and more. I would drive past bakeries and smile, knowing that they've survived over the years, serving their communities with fresh-baked products, and knowing that someday, that would be me. Baking was my passion, and I knew I'd be in a greater state of mind doing what I truly loved. On top of that, I'd be my own boss.

I submitted my resignation in January 2018. I felt so liberated. So free. Like a ton of bricks was finally removed from my shoulders. I've made note of all the conferences, classes, information sessions, and motivational books that will guide me on my journey to success. Monfriese Rum Cakes will be a force to be reckoned with.

 Cakeologist Christine Monfriese owns Monfriese Rum Cakes, an online bakery specializing in rum-infused desserts and unique gift boxes. For ten years she was a city bus driver, a job that paid well, and had great benefits and a pension plan, but Christine chose to do what she truly loves instead.

Website: https://www.monfrieserumcakes.com/

Fall Down Nine Times, Get up Ten

by Diana Jendrasch

As I stepped off the plane at age nineteen, I had no idea that my life would *never ever* be the same again. To this day, the memory of walking out the doors at the airport and seeing my father and boyfriend smiling, their hair freshly cut, haunts me. I remember sitting on my couch and asking, "Where is Mom?" only to be told she had died suddenly! They gave me a sleeping pill and sent me to bed. This life-changing event sparked the spiral of what turned out to be twenty years of complete chaos in my life. I dropped out of university, and dated one bad boyfriend after another, only to end up in an abusive marriage for over ten years. My family fell apart after the death of my mother: My father became a serial dater until he remarried a woman who hated my sister and I; my sister and I have never been able to navigate our lives successfully enough to have a relationship with each other; and then my father passed away!

How do you recover?

You struggle, you fall, and you hit rock bottom. What constitutes rock bottom? It varies for each person. I have seen several rock bottoms including receiving my divorce papers from the lawyer and being told that having three children and giving up my career to raise them entitled me to $272 a month in child support! That led me to drink so much that my current husband held back my hair as I vomited. Or, sitting alone at the police station stating I had had enough of my husband's abuse knowing that if he found out it would only escalate. Did I have a choice, any choice? I sure as hell did—I got up. With each shitty life lesson, I grew and developed a strength I never knew I had. Now, I find joy in the smallest of accomplishments and I have four *wonderful* children. Fall down nine times, get up ten!

Life is not easy—you may stumble, you may fall, but you must fight for you!

Diana Jendrasch is a positive, energetic entrepreneur and mom of four amazing kids. After a challenging divorce, Diana became passionate about personal finance. Now, as a mortgage agent and personal finance coach, she educates women on how to budget, save, and create a healthy relationship with money.

Instagram: https://www.instagram.com/pdlending/
Website: https://www.pdlending.ca/

Challenge Your Inner Critic

by Donald Brown

Empowering oneself shouldn't be merely a pursuit, but more the embracing of a new way of life. From qualifying yourself for a job to proving your worth to your toughest inner critic, taking the daily challenge of being the best version of yourself, despite the failures and misfortunes you will encounter, propels you to a state of harmony that only a small percentage of the population lives in.

By no means am I perfect, nor do I have it all worked out. What I can tell you is that I have a strong work ethic. As I've learned, a strong work ethic beats smarts any day of the week. It showcases so many strong characteristics that people can't help but admire. It gives you the foundation to master other weaknesses you may face. They may not like you, but they'll respect you in the end. Mix it with faith and ambition and you're running the right race.

I have failures every day, but my daily successes continuously strengthen my resolve to share my triumphs with everyone I'm blessed to share space with, including you. Growing up wasn't easy as we have all experienced, but I want you to relish the blessing that your own individual journey has brought you to this very place of awareness. Without that acknowledgment, you can't own your path, nor can you change the trajectory of where you go next.

My closing wish for you is this: find someone you admire, who's where you want to be and look into their life. Nothing worthwhile comes easy. Real success takes sacrifice and an unflinching desire. Find what you're willing to give up to claim the life you deserve, and empower yourself mind, body, and spirit and achieve it!

After many years in different sectors, Donald Brown stumbled into the non-profit sector, and his true calling was revealed. Now, in addition to being an inspiring speaker and coach, Donald utilizes his love of driving and helping people—specifically driving for uber—as another platform to heal and teach.

Instagram: the_don_chronicles

To Be or Not to be?
Self-Preservation

by Donna Sobers

My family often refers to me as the younger, older sister because I'm "the responsible one." Over the years I wore this title with confidence and pride but my mom's illness forced me to analyse my role and who I am.

My first responsible task came at twelve: I was appointed to deliver the news to my grandmother that my sister and I would not return to Trinidad because my mom wanted us to remain in Canada. When we started living with our parents we were exposed to a life of domestic violence, which we did not experience living with our grandparents. This dynamic changed my perception of relationships and I became my mother's defender. As a teenager, I resented the situation and also my mom for staying to keep up this façade of family.

This experience propelled me to approach my life differently. I built a persona of toughness, determined not to be trapped in the domestic violence cycle.

Life was fantastic! The Lord kept my emotions intact by sending a fantastic husband who saw through my wall and was faithful and patient with me. We created a great family and a safe, peaceful home.

Then my mom fell ill and I got into action, being strong for everyone. But my emotional stability was challenged and I began to feel overwhelmed, disconnected, and exhausted with my life. I didn't want to be responsible anymore! I figured it was God's way of saying, "I'm here. Don't try to do everything yourself."

I reached out to a friend who was a coach and I remember saying to her, "I'm everyone's outlet, but who do I turn to?" She agreed to connect with me once a week to sort out my stuff. I started journaling regularly, strengthening my relationship with God; and living in a moment of gratitude, and not trying to fix everything. With these few simple things, I was able to preserve my sanity. I let many things go that I thought were my responsibility and I learned to take care of me. Self-preservation is now my priority!

Donna Sobers is a business and event marketing specialist with an extensive portfolio in profitable and non-profit organizations. She has a reputation as a connector who is instrumental in bringing collaborative minds together to execute events. Donna is also a wife and a mother of three fantastic children.

https://www.linkedin.com/in/donna-sobers-47871156

Is Money Your Friend?

by Ewa Teresa Wozniak

Seeing money as one of your best friends is essential in order to live a fulfilled life. I was raised with a scarcity mindset about money and everything else, yet I managed to obtain my master's degree in nursing with a thesis in prevention at a university overseas. Shortly after that, I landed in Canada on Christmas Day not knowing what life would bring me and seeing a glass half empty everywhere around me. I grew up with fear, doubt, worry and distorted beliefs about money. It was failure after failure with whatever I touched until I realized that further self-discipline of a clear, focused, unlimited mindset and taking actions was the way. I believe in prevention of all unpleasant or undesired happenings for the client and the self. I see families in the community making educated financial choices, living life with purpose, and feeling peaceful about tomorrow. Financial health is the core pillar of family and business operations.

I was growing my savings until one time when I needed to help my family overseas. I took all the money I had at the time and sent it to save them. My first credit card allowed me to easily pay for things including education, but that created financial hardship when my earnings did not cover my needs, wants, and desires. Educating myself in the financial industry taught me that we must constantly monitor our finances in order to have enough. Money drives healthy relationships in the household. The same discipline guides the mind and money. Changing one thought a day can create a new reality. Saving one dollar a day accumulates 365 dollars a year and may be multiplied.

The Creator gave me what I needed to rebuild a healthy belief about money, and become its friend in a respectful, loving, and straightforward way. Despite who we are and what we do money determines our financial independence now and in the future. In spite of how my story began, I am in the financial industry where I help families and businesses have a bright and rewarding, financially-independent future.

Ewa T. Wozniak was born in Poland. After earning her master's degree in nursing from the University of Lublin, she came to Canada. Her current focus is financial health as a core pillar in family and business operations. She enjoys networking and helping clients achieve bright and rewarding financially-independent futures.

Facebook: www.facebook.com/ewatwozniak

Instagram: www.intagram.com/wozniak9510

Twitter: twitter.com/ewawozniak189

LinkedIn: linkedin.com/in/ewa-t-wozniak-49721640

My Journey: The Seven Amazing Steps That Shrunk My Uterine Fibroids

by Francisca Epale

I was diagnosed with fibroids by my medical doctor in October 1996, when I lived in the United States. She advised me that, "Fibroids are benign (non-cancerous) tumors that sometimes cause heavy menstrual periods, miscarriages, failure to conceive, and black women are more likely to have them." Years later, I read that 30 percent of all women get fibroids. I was married at the time of my diagnosis and being childless was not an easy path to follow. I was criticized, humiliated and insulted, but I left my dilemma in the hands of God.

While doing research about my condition, I consulted many different health care practitioners (homeopathic, naturopathic and gynecologists) in the United States, Canada and China. Together we developed a personal regimen that I believe contributed to the shrinkage of my fibroids. I call them the seven amazing steps:

1. Acupuncture

2. FreeMart™ health products

3. Kegel exercises, aerobics, yoga, and Pilates

4. Massage therapy

5. Specialized diet

6. Traditional Chinese Medicine

7. Reciting positive affirmations

Over the years, several medical practitioners in Canada and China recommended that I undergo a hysterectomy due to my menorrhagia (excessive bleeding) but I refused because of the side effects. Then in 2016 I sought the advice of an international naturopathic doctor who performed a biofeedback body scan on me. The machine diagnosed that due to my advanced age, a hysterectomy was unnecessary! There are alternatives to having a hysterectomy. My pain turned into a gain; my battles into blessings; and my mess into a message.

Medical Disclaimer

I am not a health practitioner. I do not cure uterine fibroids. The information contained in this chapter is based on my personal journey and is not intended to provide medical advice. The seven steps mentioned may not work for you. It is advisable to first seek advice from a medical doctor. My story is just for general information and inspiration.

 Francisca Epale, an accredited community French interpreter, has more than twenty years' experience teaching French and English in the US, China, and Canada. Author of *The Naked Educator: Secrets to Surviving in China as an Expatriate,* second edition, and an award-winning speaker, she has obtained her Distinguished Toastmasters designation (DTM).

https://www.facebook.com/francisca.epale

https://ca.linkedin.com/in/franciscaepale

I Jumped into My Next Chapter in Life with a Solid Heart!

by Gloria Morgan

Mom was in her last days of leukemia in a coma, and I was her caregiver. The father of my children treated me as a possession and was living a life of grandeur with no care for his girls or me. We were running and expanding an international food and beverage operation. He was operations in-house, and I was trademarks, joint venture, franchise, and real estate. We had already opened Sports Cafe sites in Canada (Toronto, Mississauga), South Africa (Cape Town, Durban, Johannesburg), and England (London) and had Birmingham starting to roll. We had other named venues in place as well. Our lives were busy. We used to be happy.

Standing on the edge of that bungee platform, I knew that I could no longer procrastinate about my future. I had to make a big decision. I wanted the freedom to raise my girls in a stress-free, loving, and positive environment, and I knew I could if I worked up the courage. I knew I would deal with life threats and challenges of security on many levels. I knew he would never stop trying to break me.

Fifteen minutes later, I jumped. Apparently, I broke two records: best-dressed bungee jumper and ... standing on the edge the longest and still jumping!

Yes, I became a proud single mom, started my own business, and raised two amazing girls to be strong, independent women. Yes, I am happy!

The most difficult thing in life is trying to make a decision. Courage comes from within. Understand your strength. The easiest thing in life is creating and following the path after the decision is made!

Gloria Morgan, presently representing Royal LePage, provides concierge service in real estate, including residential, investment, commercial, and leisure properties. Her background includes the positions of Director of Properties for Crown Life Insurance Company; Director of Properties for Sports Cafe International; and self-employed for design-build luxury homes.

https://www.specialneedsrealestate.com/

Be Open-minded and Optimistic

by Gregory Turner

Entrepreneurship has always been my dream. Since high school, I knew that business ownership was my destination. When I moved to Canada at the age of twenty-three, I knew very little of my new home and had no social network. I had very little experience running a business, and I felt I had no mentors who had the experience to guide me on what to do. I was wide-eyed and ambitious. I knew that having a good network of knowledgeable people around me was very important, but the big question was, how would I acquire it?

What I learned was how important it was to openly express my goals if I was serious about achieving them. When I did so, the right people and opportunities would present themselves, giving me the option to choose the best way forward. What I did next was very important.

After sharing my goals with a few people in my growing social circle, some opportunities were presented to me. At the time, they weren't what I considered ideal opportunities, however I was open-minded and willing to explore where the doors open to me would lead. This process took me way out of my comfort zone.

The opportunities opened me up to a world of personal growth, and to learning the fundamentals of operating a business that led me to where I am today—owning a software development company and a digital marketing agency. Taking those first opportunities also led to me being introduced to a broad network of professional business owners. Today I feel comfort knowing that for every challenge I have in my business, there is someone I can call who will know exactly what I should do next.

If there is one thing I want you to take from my experience, it is that sometimes your opportunities do not present themselves as you first imagined they would, but taking them is an important step in your journey that can lead you to the destination you have in mind.

 Gregory Turner is the author of the book Supersize Your Business. He is also the co-founder of Supersize Your Business, a digital marketing agency specializing in online lead generation, as well as the software company Intigent, which specializes in business intelligence applications.

Website: www.supersizeyourbusiness.ca

Twitter: https://twitter.com/SupersizeYour

Facebook: https://www.facebook.com/supersizeyourbusinessonline/

Empowered to Give

by Hadriana Leo

Have you looked inside?
What did you see?
She looked inside, saw doubt and misery
But how could that be?
She is strong, they say,
She is the sunshine that brightens their day

Well, the outside was real
But on a bad day not so
She sometimes didn't know whether to come or to go
She struggled inside
Didn't know where to turn
Didn't know what to do with that interior burn

Was she driven,
Or dreamin'?
Was this reality she was livin'?

To believe the words she must trust the speaker
But experience had taught to look beyond words, listen deeper
For to speak and then do wasn't the natural order
Of those that surrounded this special daughter.

She'd been touched where he shouldn't have,
Her life changed when it needn't have,
All without a word spoken, no balm, no salve

She kept smilin'
Time kept tickin',
One step at a time, no time for trippin'

The years passing by did not lessen the sear,
In fact it intensified, waiting for it's time to appear
To flare and blaze, even to consume
To glow in its purity and set fire to the room

The fuel came later, without any bidding
Confirming the fact that you're sent what you're needing
Distasteful, painful, the fuel was supplied
And as it poured in, she thought anymore and I'll die

But it continued to pour, to force her to taste
To force her to look, to consider without haste
She simmered, she smouldered, she sizzled and crackled
She burned so hot she melted her shackles

Her doubt fell right off when she learned the clear lesson
That her trust was best placed in the mirror's own person
And what others saw was only a glimmer
Of the magic, the mystery, the unexplainable wonder

She was driven not dreamin'
Her reality was the life she chose to be livin'
She smiled 'cause she chose to
Her drum, not the clock was the beat she marched on to,
No time for trippin' when she had life to stand up to

In all, our girl Pat, found without doubt
Your fire burns hot 'cause it's in you to give, never put out.

Hadriana Leo is The Money Navigator™. She helps couples, women, and young adults conquer the debt, doubt, and drama that is keeping them from realizing their financially-driven goals and dreams. She uses Behavioural Cashflow Planning™ techniques, combining Math+Mindset™ to create a unique solution for every client.

www.crescendofinancial.com

Unlock Your Dreams Through the Power of Manifestation

by Hanah Ahmed

I looked forward to my work commute. I loved sitting in the dedicated quiet section of the train, popping on my headset and diving into a guided meditation, which would connect me to my higher self and lead me to a blissful state. I visualized my life being so different than working as an information technology consultant at the bank. When my destination arrived my visualization and dreams would be placed on hold.

My position as a woman in technology was definitely challenging and kept me in fight or flight mode so that I continually overachieved in my work projects and delivered them prior to deadlines. I interacted with the vice presidents on a daily basis and worked really hard to maintain my reputation. But a voice within would whisper, this is all temporary, your soul has a higher purpose to serve humanity and make a positive impact in people's lives. And, after years of proving my worth and dedication in corporate I was beginning to feel unfulfilled on a soul level, and to recognize I was not living my life purpose.

Through the years I completed many healing modality certifications and worked on my spiritual component with an abundance of spiritual teachers. As I deepened my spiritual practices, I kept hearing that voice, but I feared it and the responsibility of being a spiritual teacher. It was easier to have a day job at the bank.

Today I am grateful that I listened to the whispers and have manifested the life I once only dreamt of—helping transform women's careers from corporate to their soul purpose business through motivational, transformative, and spiritual coaching.

It is through the grace of god, meditations, and years of spiritual growth that I have been led to serve others and live my life with purpose and a deep sense of satisfaction.

What is yours will find its way to you. When you feel a deep void within yourself, it's time to listen to that little whisper. It's there to serve you and lead you to a pathway of miracles that await you.

Happy manifesting!

Hanah Ahmed is a soul purpose strategist, intuitive healer, and twin flame love coach bridging the gap between today's hectic lifestyle and creating a life of balance and ease. Her light-hearted persona allows her to ignite the calm between the logical mind and the restlessness of the searching soul.

https://www.hanahahmed.com/

https://www.facebook.com/
HanahAhmedBusinessAscensionStrategist/

https://www.instagram.com/hanah.ahmed/

https://twitter.com/hanahahmed7

I Wish Someone Would Have Helped Me Make Better Financial Decisions

by Heather Holjevac

I wish someone would have helped me make better financial decisions. That's what my mother said after her divorce and my sister's nearly life-ending ski accident thirty years ago.

I saw my mother go through a divorce, lose one child and nearly another. Throughout all of this, there was no one to help her make informed financial decisions. Anyone she dealt with in the financial industry was only concerned with commissions and sales quotas, not how decisions would impact her life. When my mother was divorcing and deciding to retire early to assist my sister after her accident, no one offered to prepare a cash flow analysis or explain the future financial impact of her options. There wasn't any follow-through to make sure her funds were drawn down slowly to preserve her capital and lifestyle.

After seeing my mother's struggle with making and understanding her financial decisions with little guidance, I knew there had to be a better way for women to get the advice and resources they needed to make better financial decisions. So, I made it my life's mission to do that. At twenty, armed with ambition to make a difference, I moved to

Toronto from New Brunswick to learn all I could about the financial industry, only to discover the industry was full of conflicts of interest. How could I balance earning a living, with making a sale tied to a commission? I wanted to make it about the lives I could change—making a financial difference in my clients' lives and empowering them with financial education—not the sales I could make.

While it has been an uphill struggle over the years balancing this, fee-for-service financial planning is becoming more prevalent. Separating advice from products, and strategy from solutions, and providing a solid financial education base, helps me provide complete financial peace of mind for each client, and customize a detailed financial plan that addresses all of their needs.

It is all worthwhile when my clients thank me for helping them make better financial decisions that allow them to lead the lives they dreamed about.

Heather Holjevac, CFP, CDFA, EPC, FP Canada Fellow distinction, financial planner, and president of The Holjevac Group works to advance financial literacy. Heather helps people understand their financial options as they prepare for transition, whether it's retiring, selling their homes, or when they find themselves single or caring for aging parents.

Facebook: www.facebook.com/heatherholjevac.1

Website: www.heatherholjevac.com

LinkedIn: /heather-holjevac-cfp-cdfa-epc-b22b33a

Twitter: @heatherholjevac

Contact: info@heatherholjevac.com

Subject to Change—Mindset Matters.

by Heather Mae Cavanagh

What do you think? What do you believe? What are the thoughts that happen in the privacy of your mind?

Fact: What you think is a key source of power behind how you behave, measure your capabilities and view the experiences and people around you.

It's well documented that a fundamental difference between the madly successful and the merely mediocre is how we think about ourselves, learning and life. There is no single characteristic, learned behaviour or habit that is more powerful in determining your success than thinking prolifically and positively.

Research shows that over 90 percent of women end their days thinking about what they didn't accomplish, their doubts, fears and where they weren't good enough. Then, over 80 percent of women wake up looking for their to-do list. It's a steady and overwhelming mindset of not measuring up. We need to interrupt these thought patterns and break these habits.

How do you sort through your thoughts?

It's mindset work to spend time on your thinking and it generates powerful results. Think about athletes. They have used mindset techniques and coaches for decades to improve their performance and move past personal and situational limitations to achieve big dreams and goals.

Creating meaningful change requires insight into why you think a thought. It requires understanding into the motivations, experiences and realities that brought this thought and line of thinking to the table for you. It requires accountability to do the thinking.

We tend to focus on manipulating the results outside of us not realizing that all we have to do is shift our filters to create tangible changes and present new solutions. First seek awareness. Then you can change. Techniques such as visualization and mindset training can foster meaningful responses to any situation or behaviour that you'd like to change.

Old ways don't open new doors, so maybe it's time to take a reflective pause and refocus on what you think and the power that holds.

Your mindset is subject to change—change your mindset and subject yourself to awesome change. It's personal, it's powerful and it's going be great.

Heather Mae Cavanagh is passionate about collaborative work while seeking balance amongst motherhood, career, challenges, and happiness. She mentors others, shifting their mindset, uncovering their resilience, and improving their networking ability to make critical connection

Heather has a BA (Wilfrid Laurier University), and an MA (leadership studies, University of Guelph).

https://heathermaecoaching.com/

http://www.instagram.com/heathermaeco

https://www.facebook.com/chezheathermae

http://linkedin.com/in/chezheathermae

What if life was happening for you, not to you?

by Heather Thomson

I looked like a typical eleven-year-old, but inside I felt troubled and depressed. After my parents adopted my siblings and me, they took in thirty foster children. Luckily, I knew that I was adopted, but I never fit in. I couldn't feel my mom's love because she was dealing with past emotional trauma. Her voice saying, "I told the agency that I didn't want a child with red hair and freckles but got you," looped in my head.

Being quiet and withdrawn, I found making friends difficult. I had a deep, dark secret eating me up inside. My earliest memory of my cousin "experimenting" on me was confusing. Some of the foster boys, guys at school, and a different cousin weren't so nice.

Surprised to be invited to a birthday party, I danced and played games like drinking Coke with Aspirin. Aspirin takes pain away. I took one, three, twenty, fifty, up to eighty-six. I passed out. Running to the bathroom, a river of blood gushed from my mouth as if it were coming from a fire hose. I never told anyone. Shortly after, a powerful, strange feeling shook me and I heard a loud voice in my head. There was something to accomplish, some reason why I needed to help others.

That spiritual awakening has kept me alive for forty years, but for thirty of them I couldn't break the cycle of abuse. I searched for answers but my life resembled a roller coaster, resulting in three more attempts to take my pain away, and one near-death experience. But during dark times, I remembered that calling and survived, even though guilt and shame tormented me.

Then after I found another date's hands around my neck, I decided to do whatever was necessary to change my life. I couldn't help others if I didn't heal myself first. Attending Tony Robbins' Date with Destiny event I discovered unique skills resulting from my experiences. Transforming, I understood that life was happening for me. Now I'm fulfilling my calling by creating a not-for-profit real estate business. Life will never be the same!

Heather Thomson is a real estate investor, restaurant owner, and accountant. She is the passionate founder of Two Spirits for Change, helping abuse survivors while proudly creating her real estate business, HCJ Properties for her family. Heather's triumph over a life of adversity inspires others to empower themselves.

Website: http://www.mirtofresh.com

Website: http://www.hcjproperties.com/

Website: http://www.2spirits4change.com/

LinkedIn: www.linkedin.com/in/heatherathomson

Facebook: https://www.facebook.com/heather.thomson.3998

Where Am I

by Ian Cunningham

Let's start where I was…

I was sure of myself…
I was sure of my strength,
I was sure in what I, believed.

I knew whom I could trust…
I knew where I fit in,
I knew what I knew and, that's me.

Here's what happened…

I was told to move on…
I was told "you're no good,"
I was told that I'm not, wanted.

But I knew they were wrong…
But I knew how it worked,
But I thought that I knew, it all.

Where did it leave me?

In a place full of doubt…
In a mood full of rage,
In a struggle left for, myself.

And no one could help me…
And nowhere would hire me,
And time did nothing but, damage.

What happened to me?

It took me two years to…
Get back on my feet and,
I thought into what I, wanted.

But something was missing…
But something was empty,
But where did my confi, dence go?

The next little while…

I played like I should have…
I tried not to falter,
I did a good job so, I thought.

I didn't feel proud though…
I didn't feel pleasure,
I did not like what I'd, become.

Where did that leave me?

Still looking for hope and…
Still looking for change and,
Still looking for proof I, belonged.

Then chance played a part when…
A chance meeting happened,
A chance to make change that, I needed.

What did I do next?

I listened to words and…
I listened to phrases,
I listened like never, before.

I realized the truth and…
I realized the problem,
I realized it's me that, must change.

Where do I take it?

I go forward, equipped…
I go forward, less hurt,
I go forward because, I'm loved.

I'll listen to others…
I'll take what is needed,
I'll pass on this knowledge, to you.

What do I know now?

I know I'm still hurting…
I know I'm still struggling,
I know I am scared but, alright.

As long as I'm focused…
As long as I'm trying,
I know I can fail—and—succeed!

Ian Cunningham is an award-winning radio writer and producer with over twenty-five years of broadcasting experience. Currently, Ian is the founder and principle of Thought Radar, where he inspires people through the power of "perspective thinking" as a public speaker and life coach.

Website: https://www.thoughtradar.ca

Instagram: https://www.instagram.com/radar_cunningham/

From a Rocky Start to an Odd Turning Point

by Isabelle Anaelle

I was fortunate to be born and to grow up in gorgeous France until I finished university. And in fact, looking back, I have been blessed with great luck from birth. However, I felt hardship for decades.

When I was seven years old, my parents divorced, and my dad became a single dad of three. As the oldest child of a traditional Asian family, I had to assume responsibility early on to help with cleaning, cooking, and raising my siblings. At that age, I was also slapping myself because I thought I was ugly. At twelve, I was writing poems about death. In fact, as a child and well into my adulthood, I often had morbid sadness, feelings of abandonment, and pessimism.

During my youth my diet was not the best, with a predilection for rich French foods and sweets, yet not worse than today's typical North American diet laden with processed and unnatural foods. I used to experience chronic hay fever, hives, heartburn, canker sores, constipation, bad digestion, bloating, bronchitis, and lack of energy, which I discovered much later are all symptoms of acidity and inflammation, very common nowadays. Until my early twenties, when

I became physically more active, I would sometimes cry from back pain preventing me from sitting, walking, or doing activities for too long.

Despite material abundance, my personal life was dampened by relationship drama, and also by the boredom of a lack of purpose and direction. Eventually, I felt increasingly trapped in an unhealthy marriage, and weakened by a lack of courage and financial co-dependence. How could I transcend my fear, uncertainty, and anxiety to visualize a brighter future, happiness, and total health for myself?

Well, besides deeply thanking my dear dad for raising and providing us with strict but good moral values, I praise the miracle of a particular but odd turning point, when serendipity connected me to what I call my guidance within or my higher self. This was, I believe, the spark for my spiritual and evolutionary shift! It eventually led me to love myself into natural and holistic health.

Isabelle Anaelle is the founder of Bio+Sources, which offers people and health-food stores 100% pure whole foods supplements with a high life force. They support health and increase energy levels, naturally and holistically. She is also a certified Reconnective Healing® Practitioner, Thetahealer®, lymphologist, and holds a master's in economics.

https://bio-sources.com/
https://www.biochlorella.com/
https://www.facebook.com/Bio-Chlorella-244025992438805/
https://www.instagram.com/biochlorella/
https://www.pinterest.ca/biochlorella3/
https://twitter.com/biochlorellacom
https://biochlorella.tumblr.com/

Connecting to My Guidance Within

by Isabelle Anaelle

My spiritual birth happened one lucky day, just after I discovered and received a chi session to raise the energy of my prolapsed bowel. At that time, I was also dabbling in better nutrition to enhance my digestion and elimination processes, as I needed to lose the thirty pounds I had gained. To my surprise, I felt a magical sensation that initiated a gradual shift within me, enabling me ever since to experience the companionship of this delightful life energy moving, and almost dancing, throughout my body!

What was this miraculous life force inside? Where was this higher intelligence coming from? How did it know exactly how to stretch me, ease the pain, and shape my body, while also guiding me towards wise and creative answers? Flabbergasting! In fact, this energy field emanates from our inner life-force, our higher self; it exists in all of us. Every day I am thankful and in awe to be connected to it. It's like being perfectly guided by my own internal global positioning system (IGPS) and best friend simultaneously!

My higher self helps me to grow through and from tough times; to get the lessons and learning; to listen to the inner voice of my authentic self, passions and life purpose; and to discover remarkable short-cut tools to help me create the healthy body, mind, and soul, and the life I truly desire, at all levels. It's an ongoing transformative blessing!

As a result, I've been able to remove a lot of debris that was no longer serving me; to completely change my life and my environment; to learn how to become self-sufficient and independent; and to feel much happier, freer and healthier than ever before. All this while following my passion for natural health and anti-aging, through the lenses of energy, frequency, vibration, and quantum field.

I also became a certified lymphologist, theta healer, and reconnective healing foundational practitioner, and continuously explore energy tools and modalities. My holistic healing path has also buoyed my mission to elevate other people's health and energy field through Bio+ Sources, the natural wellness company I created.

Isabelle Anaelle is the founder of Bio+Sources, which offers people and health-food stores 100% pure whole foods supplements with a high life force. They support health and increase energy levels, naturally and holistically. She is also a certified Reconnective Healing® Practitioner, Thetahealer®, lymphologist, and holds a master's in economics.

https://bio-sources.com/
https://www.biochlorella.com/
https://www.facebook.com/Bio-Chlorella-244025992438805/
https://www.instagram.com/biochlorella/
https://www.pinterest.ca/biochlorella3/
https://twitter.com/biochlorellacom
https://biochlorella.tumblr.com/

Loving Ourselves into Health in These Challenging Times

by Isabelle Anaelle

We face challenging times that threaten our physical, mental, and spiritual health because of the growing chaos; broken families; disorientation; pollution; natural disasters; illnesses; chemically-laden foods; and economic and healthcare worries that the world is facing. Following natural restorative ways to feed our cells; detoxify holistically; enhance our lymphatic systems; and harmonize our vibration fields, are simple, economical, yet intelligent and multi-beneficial answers that can catapult us towards awesome health and life changes! They offer a portal to true service for us to create our better tomorrow more effortlessly.

For example, taking advantage of the immense goodness of Mother Nature, particularly through whole and natural foods with high vibration, is an easy and economical gateway to better nourishment, health, and cleaner blood. Furthermore, such foods may also lead to higher planes for manifestation and abundance. Indeed, over time, you might notice that you develop smarter thoughts, have deeper intuition, and make wiser choices and decisions, among other benefits. Dwelling in the powerful effects of detoxifying and freeing yourself from energy blockages and accumulated toxins, whether at a physical, emotional, energetic, or spiritual level, could also work miracles to empower and shift your health and reality.

More than ever, enhancing our physical, mental, and spiritual health should be at the forefront of everyone's pursuit. I urge you to increase your consciousness about energy medicine and about what is naturally good for you. Spend the time to educate yourself as there is no better return on investment. Truly love yourself into health by honoring your precious organs, brain, mind, and life force. Prevent them from degenerating with thoughtful choices; don't allow yourself to become the victim of harmful foods and meds!

Everything is energy. So, if you want to raise your vibration, you need to be mindful and remember that everything you feed your cells, your mind, and your spirit has an effect on your energy field. In fact, refining your personal frequency and vibration is of utmost importance; it's an elevator to the dreams and happier reality you deserve to create; and to helping others.

How awesome is your rainbow?

 Isabelle Anaelle is the founder of Bio+Sources, which offers people and health-food stores 100% pure whole foods supplements with a high life force. They support health and increase energy levels, naturally and holistically. She is also a certified Reconnective Healing® Practitioner, Thetahealer®, lymphologist, and holds a master's in economics.

https://bio-sources.com/
https://www.biochlorella.com/
https://www.facebook.com/Bio-Chlorella-244025992438805/
https://www.instagram.com/biochlorella/
https://www.pinterest.ca/biochlorella3/
https://twitter.com/biochlorellacom
https://biochlorella.tumblr.com/

A Second Chance

by Ivanka Siolkowsky

I remember it like it was yesterday—waking up on the floor, disoriented, surrounded by empty pill bottles, crinkled up Kleenex, and a photo of my family covered in dried tears. My vision was fuzzy and my memory hazy, but eventually I realized what had happened: I could now add suicide to the long list of things I wasn't good at—another life failure in the most ironic sense.

"Suicide is so selfish! Didn't you think of how this would affect your family, your students…your dying mother?"

Of course I did, that's all I thought about, but in that moment the pain from my depression and anxiety took over and there was only one way out. To this day, I can't explain the power of that exact moment when I decided to take my own life, or how those thoughts negated anything else of value in it. They just did.

The pain that comes with mental illness, and the inability to control your own thoughts is exhausting, so I needed to find that control somewhere else…and I did. I discovered that in order to counteract the clutter in my brain, I needed to declutter the physical space around me. By doing that, I found an inner peace and level of productivity that I didn't know existed.

Did my mental illness disappear? No, that hasn't changed. What changed in me was the day I decided to honour God's will and use that second chance I'd been given to make a difference.

So here I am. I've channeled my anxiety and obsessive-compulsive disorder into a successful professional organizing business called The Tidy Moose. I've written and illustrated a children's book and created a program to help youth get organized and live with fewer material possessions, which helps their development and lowers their anxiety. My mission is to help others declutter their way to inner peace.

The trick to life is not just using the gifts you've been given, but also to turn what you've deemed a curse into the most powerful gift of all.

Ivanka Siolkowsky, a former teacher, diagnosed with depression, anxiety, and obsessive-compulsive disorder (OCD) in her early twenties, has experienced many life challenges. She faced her demons straight on by starting her own business as a professional organizer and now devotes her time to helping others find inner peace through organization.

www.tidymoose.com

Lessons from a Common Cold

by Jan Miller

Christmas 2016. I can't remember the last time a cold hung around for more than a day. I am flat on my back, wrapped in blankets with my teeth chattering. What is the lesson in this? What is the blessing in this?

I have been eating clean. I have released 30 pounds. I exercise more than I used to. Okay, not enough, but more than before. I have done everything right over the past few months. So why am I flat on my back?

The lesson is that stuff happens—even when you do everything right. What's important is how you live your life every day. Tony Robbins says, "It's not what we do once in a while that shapes our lives. It's what we do consistently." So keep eating clean. Keep releasing the weight. Keep exercising. Honour your body and honour your rituals. Yes, you might get knocked flat, but you can always work your way back up and start moving forward.

The blessing is that stuff happens—even when you do everything right. The blessing is that there are people willing to help—like your Mom coming in at three o'clock in the morning to wrap a snuggly blanket around your feet so that they finally get warm and you finally get some rest. You are not alone. The blessing is the humility of knowing that you can't be perfect because, well, stuff happens. The blessing is that you are forced to pause and honour your body. So, sip your tea. Read a good book. Take a long nap. Gently stretch and get back up.

Like my Christmas cold, stuff happens—even when you do everything right. The ultimate lesson and blessing is that you get to choose how you react. You can choose the Universe's message to slow down, or you can fight it every step of the way. As for me, there is a cup of tea, a warm blanket, and an open book waiting. Blessings to you and to your choice.

Jan Miller is a business consultant and life coach. With over three decades working with multi-national teams and through countless personal development trainings, she has developed the tools to facilitate communication at all levels of education and skills. Jan's primary goals are traveling the world and helping others enjoy success.

Note to Self: Just Show Up, Be You, and Rock it!

by Janet Charette

I was at a writers workshop in Toronto, Feb. 22, 2017 and I was listening to my coach Odette say just write, don't edit, whatever you write will be perfect.

What was in me that it had to be perfect? Was I afraid to shine? Was I afraid of my own harsh, internal critic if I messed up? My mess was my message, right? It wasn't about me winning a Pulitzer, it was about me giving others hope. Teach my children to pray, teach my children to

play, right? It wasn't about me, right? Bullshit! It was all about me and me getting out of my own way.

Write 350 words. Answer three questions. What was your defining moment? How did that

make you feel? What happened after that?

I was 350 words away from being a published author and everything I thought I wanted, and I was frozen! Welcome to my private hell. This was my umpteenth workshop, I'd spent so much money on self-help, and I had been this close so many times before this moment. Now, on February 22, 2017, while the veterans and the First Nations were taking a stand for Standing Rock, I chose to take a stand for me, no matter what!

Vignettes of my past challenges were flashing in front of me like a telenovela: fifteen years of a medicated, suicidal, bipolar depression; electroshock therapy; head-on collision; widowed once from asbestosis; widowed twice from diabetes and chronic obstructive pulmonary disease; repaying the bank $1.2 million; surviving being audited and fined by Canada Revenue Agency; having my wages garnished ...

Nothing I had faced had prepared me for what was happening to me as I stared at that blank page. Sheer terror! I felt like my stomach was going to implode if I dared to write, if I dared to dream. But in that moment, I realized that overcoming writer's block was loving myself enough to fail. I wrote the chapter! Self-compassion, forgiveness, and self-acceptance were the tools I used to finally jump, and the cliff disappeared.

Once upon a time, Janet Charette did everything possible to fit into what she thought was the perfect box. Then life woke her up and she realized there is no box, there is only love. She now spends her life being herself and teaching people how to set themselves free.

Master Thetahealing® Instructor

https://www.thetahealing.com/theta-specialist-profile.html?id=52961

https://www.facebook.com/travelingthetahealer/

http://travelingthetahealer.com/

Master Compassionkey Coach

janetc@compassionkey.com

compassionkey.com/JanetC

After the Doorbell Rang

by Janet Heidker

10:00 p.m. March 11, 2007. I was alone. I had taken a bath, put on my housecoat, and begun watching TV when the doorbell rang. I opened the door to a young, black female. She stood back and two masked men, one pointing a gun, forced their way into my home. One threw me against the wall and said, "Give me your jewellery and money NOW." I was so scared I said I didn't have any cash, so he threw me down my basement stairs.

My thoughts raced as I lay there on the floor, my back aching. This can't be happening to me. But you know what? Bad things happen to good people. I resolved that I wouldn't lose consciousness and that they would steal as little as possible.

They found my debit card and demanded my PIN number. I gave them the wrong number, so the tall man dragged me into the laundry room and kicked me as I lay on my back. He put his foot on my stomach and took out a pair of handcuffs. When I saw them, I kicked with both feet against his arm, and they flew into the darkness. In a rage, because I fought back, he beat me. For the next hour, the men shouted, taunted, and swore at me. Because I would not cooperate, they finally dragged me to my safe and said, "If you don't open this fucking safe, we'll blow your brains out."

I hyperventilated. As a widow, I couldn't leave my daughter an orphan, so I opened the safe. They stole money and memories and then dragged me to a bench by the back door and made me sit. The tall one said, "Take that, you bitch!" as he pistol-whipped my ear, spewing blood. I screamed, and then they ran out the door.

My wounds healed, but the subsequent years in court taught me to be mentally tough, and to never open the door to strangers. I also learned to live in the moment; don't spoil a good today by thinking about a bad yesterday.

Janet Heidker is currently a new club formation chairperson within the Toastmasters organization in Toronto. She believes that the advancement of society is based upon the advancement of women.

Tough Times Never Last,
But Tough People Do

by Jasma Thomson

I was raised by one of the strongest women you will ever meet. She fought through discrimination, prejudices, abuse, you name it, and has conquered her fears and achieved her dreams on countless levels. I'm very proud to be the youngest of two daughters to Ms. Heather Thomson.

My name is quite unique, and I like to think so am I. I was born to a teenage mother and spent the first part of my life in a shelter with my sister, who is one year older than me. We escaped from our abusive father and were seeking a new life. My sister was my guardian angel, protecting me all those years when our mother had to work around the clock in order to provide for us. My sister is kind, non-judgmental, and thanks to her I have found my calling today: to spread my passion of nonviolence toward all living beings. My second guardian angel (how lucky am I to have two?) is my grandmother, Judith Lafleur. She endured more pain in a lifetime than one can fathom, yet I have never seen her without a smile on her face and a hug to give to everyone she meets!

As a teenager I was lost in life. I did not feel the purpose or calling that I thought I should have, and I struggled with that until at age eighteen I gave birth to my beautiful daughter, Jaeda. I am grateful to her because from the moment I learned of her presence I knew I had to turn my life around and create a strong future for us. I went from not attending classes to honour student. I have joined my mother and grandmother as entrepreneurs in building a family business and not-for-profit. I am fortunate to now be at a place in my life where I can give back to my community and share my experiences to inspire those around me.

Jasma Thomson is a full-time executive assistant for an investment firm and a social activist with a commitment to supporting animal welfare and guiding youth to become leaders. Her favorite pastimes include sharing quality moments with her daughter and sharing her love of health and fitness.

Website: http://www.hcjproperties.com

Website: http://www.2spirits4change.com

My Story

by Jennilynn Chaput

It was a cold winter's day, and I was five years old standing in the hallway with my uncle getting ready to put on my pink snowsuit. I was so excited to play outside. As he was pulling up my pink pants, that's when it happened. He touched me. I stood there frozen as we stared at each other without a word spoken. This is where my journey began.

For several years I kept this secret until one day I felt the need to tell someone. And I did. My secret became public. My family was not happy with me. I was twelve, and my father, brother, and I were no longer welcomed by my mother's side of the family. I had shamed them. At school, kids called me a liar. When it came time to go to court, I could no longer speak; I had lost my voice. I was scared, alone, feeling so guilty, and blaming myself for the turmoil. I broke the family and couldn't bear to see my cousins lose their father, couldn't bear to cause any more pain. I just wanted it all to end. To go away.

From then on, I lived in shame, guilt, anger, blame, fear, and uncertainty. I carried this for forty years. Accepting unhealthy behaviours in relationships was the norm for me. I thought it was what I deserved. Then after many years of feeling lost, disconnected, and powerless, I was guided to the world of spiritual healing. Synchronicities were happening everywhere. I knew this was where I needed to be, and

I dove right in. Through years of emotional healing, personal growth, and spiritual development, I have reconnected with my inner goddess, and now I allow the light within to shine through.

Each and every one of us has value. We also have a purpose no matter how big or how small. When we find value in ourselves, we will find our purpose. Allow yourself permission to make the needed changes in order to transform your life. You are more powerful than you think!

Jennilynn Chaput is passionate about self-discovery, spiritual growth, and the mysteries of human consciousness. Coming from a dysfunctional family and unhealthy relationships, she found her purpose through emotional healing, NLP coaching, and hypnosis. She now inspires women to step back into their power to live a more meaningful, fulfilling life.

Website: https://jennilynnchaput.ca/

Contact: jennilynn@jennilynnchaput.ca

A Small but Powerful Act

by Jeremiah Belknap

My grandfather, a locksmith, often went to the roughest places in Buffalo, New York to help customers—places that no one else would go. As a World War II veteran, the dangerous neighborhoods didn't scare him; he believed everyone deserved kindness and respect. I carry those lessons with me today.

In November 2017, I was asked to lead National Grid crews in the monumental task of restoring power to Puerto Rico after Hurricane Maria hit. I didn't hesitate. Having served our nation in the military since 1995, I thought I was prepared, yet I was shocked at the extent of Maria's destruction. We basically started from scratch. Our team worked diligently for sixteen hours a day to make sure we were making a difference on a daily basis.

For 109 days the people we met had no power or running water, however they were still smiling. Every day we were inspired by their resiliency; they took the destruction in stride. Four weeks into our mission, I heard that there was a ninety-three-year-old World War II veteran in the area, military intelligence specialist, Master Sergeant Gilberto Arquinzoni-Ofray. I decided that I wanted to meet him, hear any stories he would be willing to share, and thank him for his service to our nation.

We exchanged words of gratitude. He was so thankful that I had taken the time to visit him. Gilberto reminded me of my grandfather, and I went back to his house to speak with him a couple of times before we left to come home. We shared stories and became friends. In a subsequent conversation I learned that Master Sergeant Arquinzoni-Ofray will be awarded the Bronze Star by Congress for his valor during combat.

This was a powerful moment for me, and it made me cry. This man was so appreciative of such a small gesture of gratitude, of not being forgotten, yet in reality, it meant so much to me. That's the thing about kindness; while people believe it's benefitting the receiver, it really and truly blesses the person who chooses to give.

Born and raised in Buffalo NY, Jeremiah Belknap works at National Grid. Jeremiah recently retired from the military where he served in the U.S. Navy before joining the Air Force reserves. He recently graduated with an MBA and looks forward to continuing to mentor his peers at National Grid.

www.tailormadedj.net

My Mother's Truth

by Jessica De Serre Boissonneault

Do not wait to tell your loved ones how much they are loved. Hug your mother a little tighter, kiss your daughter goodnight, and whisper I love you just one more time. We've heard these words far too often but the reality stands: tomorrow is never promised.

As a child, I recall my mother leaving me often in my grandmother's care so that she could pursue her education and career. She always did the best she could. She had me at a very young age, nineteen to be exact. We can all imagine how scary that must have been—to give life when you are nearly a child yourself. For years as a young girl reoccurring questions would cross my mind: "Am I wanted?" "Was I a mistake?" "Am I truly loved?" Little did I know that these uncertainties would carry into my adult life and that it would take the death of a loved one and thirty-one years before I would receive the answer I had chased for so long. Little did I know that it was that very answer that I needed to transform my life.

In January 2018, two years after my grandmother's death, I finally gained the courage to have a heart-to-heart with my mother. To my surprise, my mother opened up and shared that she had experienced complications throughout her pregnancy that led doctors to think that she might never be able to conceive again. She had always wanted to be a mother. The thought of not being one was enough for her to put her studies aside, quit smoking, and commit to bed rest. Nothing was going to get in the way of her having me. She loved me so deeply before she had even laid eyes on me. I was her miracle.

Today, I am forever grateful to have heard my mother's truth. Today, I get to encourage, inspire, and empower other women and mothers to speak their own truths. Don't wait another day to tell your loved ones how important they are; you have no idea how your words will impact them.

Now a proud mom of a wonderful daughter, Jessica De Serre Boissonneault is pursuing her passion of empowering women to create their lives by design. Using her positivity and absolute desire for serving, Jessica is certainly a woman you deserve to learn from.

https://www.instagram.com/ms.jessicadsb/

Heavy Is the Head That Wears the Crown

by Jey Jeyakanthan

Ever since I was a kid, I was told I could do anything, be anything and have anything. So, I dreamt of that Ferrari and hoped for that mansion. That is, until I grew older and reality dawned.

I was in my late teens when suddenly I had crazy mood swings, dizziness, and was feeling weak. I did not need a pregnancy test to tell me I was pregnant! Knocked up at 18! "Bravo!" The girl whom everybody thought would be the first to make it, the girl every parent told their child to emulate was pregnant. I purchased a pregnancy kit and asked for instructions on how to use it. Two lines!

Keeping the baby or not would be a hard decision to make. I didn't want to make the wrong decision for the wrong reasons—selfish ones. Fortunately, or unfortunately, I never had to decide; my fate was decided for me. A week later, I had a miscarriage.

Most people do not think of miscarriages as good. To me it wasn't, but it took away a decision I did not want to make! It took away the problem at hand and it was a chance to redeem myself. It was a second chance from God. I had become someone I did not respect. I had been caught up in all the stupid campus rituals. It was a slap in the face that served as a wakeup call. I knew though, that the incident had been for my own good. Instead of breaking me, it made me stronger and wiser. It made me more determined to get my success, and more importantly, I knew which road never to go down.

After that, I stayed on the straight and narrow. I made sure I would never be faced with such an awful dilemma again. I now have a beautiful family and wonderful children. Had this not happened, I don't think I would be the mother I am today. I am grateful I had a second chance, though at times I have mourned the loss of what could have been.

 Jey Jeyakanthan is a highly successful entrepreneur and IT professional. He has over twenty-two years' experience in business development and managing business transformation for Fortune-200 companies. Jey is also an active volunteer, a director of Sophia Hilton Foundation of Canada, and an active contributor to the local political arena.

Contact: jey@avaj.ca

Website: www.avaj.ca

Embrace it. Learn from it. Grow from it.

by Johanna Komar

"Stop in your pursuit of happiness, and just *be* happy…"

Understanding this changed my life. This sentence alone, when fully digested, saved me from a life of depression, drugs, and alcohol. It led me to a life of sobriety; a life of worth, excitement, and unlimited abundance.

I was looking for anything to help me feel alive in my day-to-day. But I now understand that everything we are looking for in life is not found "out there." Everything we are looking for in life is already inside should we choose to accept the challenge of regaining what is rightfully ours.

To find enrichment takes dedication. It takes dissecting your current way of existence, starting with your limiting beliefs and negative thought patterns that you probably don't even realize are harming you. It takes catching your destructive words and changing them to uplifting ones on cue. It takes ripping apart everything you've learned and have been told to be true and connecting to your inner guidance for innate wisdom. It takes fighting for your inner guru who you've been taught to believe is wrong and won't fit in with society's norms.

It takes a hell of a lot of mindful work, but my sweet God, it is worth it when it becomes your natural way of living.

You've heard it all many times before, but I'll say it again: happiness is a choice. Every second of every day, you get to choose how what happens to you will affect you. The struggles that happen to you are really no one's fault but your own for the simple fact that you allow them to be so. Realize that everything is neutral until you judge it and place a good or bad label on it. All the negativity that we perceive is just a point of reference for what we don't want, and we in turn get to take that gift and move toward something more positive.

Stop acting oblivious to the gift of polarity. Use it to your advantage to build the prosperous life you envision.

 Johanna Komar is a life skills strategist who helps you unearth your infinite potential. She uses spiritual wisdom from her past struggles to empower you to realize there's a way out of darkness. Negativity is inevitable, and she teaches you how to embrace it to increase your quality of life.

www.emergyng-energy.com

@johannakomar

My Journey to Help Moms to Fitness

by Joy Rowlandson

When I was pregnant with my first child, I was concerned about maintaining my health and physical fitness. My doctor told me that pretty much all I could do was go for walks, but that didn't satisfy me. I knew there was more I could do, but I couldn't find anyone willing to guide me through it. I wanted to learn, but there was a void of resources to learn it.

That is why, after my baby was born, I decided to pursue a personal training certification. I learned a lot about the health and capabilities of the body, and the exercises that tone and shape the muscles. I further extended my study to include pre and post-natal fitness and learned about the effects of child rearing on the body and how one can recover.

I felt there was a need for essential fitness for new mothers, and for all women in general. I also had a thirst to help women better themselves and reach for greater goals. So, I expanded my credentials to include yoga and kickboxing, and by the time my second child was born, I was teaching classes of mothers how to effectively and safely exercise, to their benefit and the benefit of their child. While caring for a newborn baby, I continued my efforts through long hours and sleepless nights and obtained my Bellies Inc. certification. This gave me an even deeper understanding of the trauma a mother's body underwent during childbirth, and what action could be taken to properly address it.

By then, I was ready to take the plunge; I left my job in the dental field and started my own business. I now train women, mothers, and mothers-to-be in the comfort of their own homes, helping them strive for and reach new goals they never before thought they could achieve. Now they are all capable of achieving their own personal joy.

Joy Rowlandson is a certified fitness trainer specializing in prenatal and postnatal women aged thirty-five to forty-five. She holds additional certifications as a core specialist; nutrition and weight-loss specialist; level-3 fitness kickboxing instructor; and as an instructor for yoga, kids' yoga, and prenatal and postnatal yoga.

www.personaljoy.ca

Love, Hope, Faith and Now, Happiness

by Judith Lafleur

Throughout my life, I have never given up hope, and I hope that you will do the same! Everyone has problems and experiences that they may wish to forget, but don't give up on your dreams. Good things happen when you least expect it.

My father was an alcoholic who could never be trusted. Drunk or sober, I had to deal with his mental and physical cruelty. Despite my father's example, I met a wonderful man. One day, he surprised my mother and I when he said that he loved me and that he was going to get a divorce. Unaware that he was married, I almost fell over.

He was separated from his wife, but then he discovered that she had been diagnosed with a brain aneurysm. For years he was torn between staying with her to take care of his first two children, or staying with me, the woman he loved. During this time, we had two children. Unfortunately, we could not take care of them and were forced to give them up for adoption. My heart was broken, but deep down, I believed that we would be reunited one day.

Almost forty years later, I got a call that changed my entire life. My daughter found me! Meeting for the first time, to my delight, she brought her two daughters and my great-grandchildren. I surprised her with her sister, brother, father, and my mother. Then, I found my first son, and my family was back together! I hear from my son during every special occasion. My daughter and I are inseparable, working on a business together. I no longer cry tears of sadness; instead, I smile daily. Through faith, this reunion has brought my whole family so much love and happiness. My dream has finally come true.

Judith Lafleur is a feisty, passionate, and tenacious businesswoman and mother of four. She escaped the abuse of an alcoholic father, reunited with her estranged family, and created a world of love and compassion around her while inspiring others never give up their hopes and dreams.

Website: http://www.mirtofresh.com
Website: http://www.hcjproperties.com/
Website: http://www.2spirits4change.com/

Finding Purpose by Looking Within

by Juliet Williams

Finding life's purpose is so important for one's livelihood. Now, as an entrepreneur, I look back on who I was when I had a great job, which paid me a great salary. Through that experience, I learned that it is more important to pursue life with purpose than continue to pursue the things that my salary afforded me. I realized that money gave me the ability to purchase and maintain a great lifestyle, but it was not a purposeful one.

The entrepreneurial spirit has always been in me as I come from a family of entrepreneurs. Growing up, my parents earned income from many sources, and as a child, I was always encouraged to make use of my skills. My mother was a teacher, and my father worked as an administrator. However, they had many other sources of income whether it was from the excellently tailored suits my father made for himself and other men in the community, or from the sale of livestock or produce from his farm.

One afternoon, I hosted a gathering at my home and was sharing my conflict with my job and finding purpose. One of my friends, who was a school administrator, reminded me of my great teaching skills and offered me an opportunity to teach night school. After pondering the thought, I decided to take up her offer. Life went in a different direction on my path to finding purpose. I quickly learned that I could live without a salary; however, I am not saying that one does not need income because we live in a monetary world. Now, I make use of skills as an educator and a REALTOR® in providing meaningful services to people and watching their lives transform, in addition to earning an income.

Today, my friends, family, and former co-workers admire how graciously I surrendered the corporate life and have not looked back. My new lifestyle has also enabled me to embrace winter activities, which I once dreaded. I share this story to encourage and inspire those who are currently in the place that I was fifteen years ago.

Juliet Williams is a Toronto-based businesswoman, educator, and real estate professional. She is always learning from every person she interacts with, and as they motivate her, she strives to empower them in return. Along with writing, Juliet also enjoys traveling, hiking, dancing, and reading.

https://thejulietwilliams.com/

https://twitter.com/julietrealtor

Karen's Journey

by Karen Prince

My journey as an entrepreneur started in a unique way. I spent seven years as an accounts receivable clerk, and then one day in 1999 I was sitting at my desk when I heard a voice telling me to quit my job because I was meant to be a businesswoman. I laughed. As strange as it seemed I asked, "What kind of businesswoman?" The voice got louder and told me to quit immediately because I was supposed to become a hairstylist.

I immediately typed my resignation letter and gave it to my boss. She could not believe I was resigning after investing seven years of hard work in my career and refused to accept the letter. I told her I had not intended to leave, but I felt a tug on my heart to pursue a new career.

I felt badly for my boss because I knew that it wasn't easy to find reliable people, so I offered a solution. I told her about a friend that I had worked with for three years in a similar positon who was looking for work. Her work ethic was as strong as mine, so I offered to call her to see if she would be interested in coming for an interview. To make a long story short, my friend came in for the interview and was offered the job on the spot!

After I left, I enrolled full time at a hairstyling school. A year later, I became a certified hairstylist and gained experience at two salons. After two years, in 2001, I opened my very own salon, which I appropriately named after myself—Salon Ka Pri.

This endeavor would prove challenging. I had to find salon space in a convenient location that was accessible by transit and car, and that would accommodate the clientele I wanted to attract. It took a couple of moves, and some lean times but I did it! Thank God I listened to that voice so many years ago. It was risky, but my persistence paid off.

In 1999, Karen Prince left her full-time job to pursue her entrepreneurial dream. She opened Salon Ka Pri in 2001 at Davenport and Dupont in Toronto. Due to an overwhelming increase in clientele, she relocated Salon Ka Pri to Vaughan in 2009. Karen's vision is to mentor up-and- coming hairstylists.

Instagram: https://www.instagram.com/salon_kapri/

Facebook: https://www.facebook.com/karen.prince.9809

Website: http://www.salonkapri.com/

Contact: salonkapri@hotmail.com

Faith and Surrender: A Story of Letting Go and Letting God

by Karla Lang

One fateful drive when I was twenty-seven years old changed my life forever. I was moving through Montreal in the pouring rain. The wipers were going at top speed, and it was still hard to see. I was driving way too fast for the conditions, but I had a car on my tail and a tractor-trailer and guard rail on either side. There was nowhere to go. All of a sudden, my car hit a large pond of water, and I started hydroplaning. My car was sliding sideways directly into the side of the truck.

I knew that if I turned the wheel, there was a chance of overcorrecting and spinning out of control, and if I didn't, I could be decapitated. Amazingly I was calm, I knew I could do nothing to change my situation, and I surrendered my fate. I literally threw my arms in the air and took my foot off the gas. I looked up to the heavens and said, "If this is how I am to die, I am yours to take." I had no fear, just trust, and so I let go of the wheel and let God. I looked down at the steering wheel, and there it was, turning itself back into safety, into the center of my lane. The truck had moved beyond me, and the car behind me had disappeared. I started laughing with joy exclaiming, thank you!

I am not suggesting that in the face of an accident, you let go of the wheel. I'm saying that what changed my life in that moment was the awareness that there is a divine presence looking out for us at all times. I learned that in the moment where I completely surrendered with faith, I was guided in the right direction and brought to the next step on my journey. I let go of what I could do and let God do it for me. Today, this insight is the guiding force for my coaching practice, where I help women to live in the flow of grace, ease, and abundance

Karla Lang is committed to helping professional women live their best career life—confident, respected, and valued as leaders; and making the money they deserve, the feminine way. Karla, CEO of LivLove, loves living in the country, being a mom of three, and owning a dog and a cat.

www.livlove.ca

Life Experiences

by Karlene Linton-Wilson

Everything in life is an experience, a lesson, or a redirection of our paths. As young women, we struggle to be accepted by our peers, our families, and society. From my teens through to adulthood I struggled with people making comments, telling me I wasn't good enough, or that I wouldn't get my goal. Women today still struggle with this. We all need to acknowledge and believe that we are enough. Once we do, we become unstoppable. Don't let anyone tell you who or what you should be. Be confident in who you are and how you look as you are beautiful inside and out.

Accept and love who you are. We have all the riches in the world, but sometimes we just can't see it. We allow so many other factors to influence us that it distracts us from our true paths. Keep your vision clear and don't listen to naysayers. Have they achieved what they want in life?

Know that whatever you want is right in front of you and you just need to reach out and grab it. Take the action needed to get what you want and release the fear attached. I am currently working on my relationship with food to reach my weight goals, and I continue to push through what look like barriers but are actually challenges to help me along the way.

I truly believe that everything happens for a reason. It really is about staying strong, confident, and knowing that there will be bumps in the road, which is ok. In the end, it's about the mindset you hold that helps to determine the results once the road clears. The Universe and God will give you what you focus on, therefore, when you focus on the negative that's what you receive. Focus on the positive and the universe will open up.

I'm still on my journey. When I feel uneasy, I remember that my current situation does not define me: I am not what happened to me; I am what I choose to become in life, love and beyond.

 Karlene Linton-Wilson is an HR professional who has recently taken on other ventures in expanding her portfolio. She is an aspiring consultant/coach. Her journey is just beginning but keep an eye out as she's looking to do great things.

mythirtyone.ca/karlie

legalshield.com/hub/klintonwilson

A Woman's Worth

by Karlene Millwood

In a world where we are constantly bombarded with negative messages, it is vitally important for women to know who they are and to intrinsically understand their worth. There is a fallacy being perpetuated that when someone exhibits a certain level of confidence, they're being arrogant. It never ceases to amaze me that those who propagate this myth are themselves insecure. When insecurity meets confidence, it labels it cockiness. If you ever encounter this; just give them your best smile and continue to be you. Confidence never answers to ignorance.

If you don't value yourself, you will teach other people not to value you either. Carry yourself in such a way that they have to respect you even if they don't like you. You are royalty! Even if your current life situation is unfavorable, it cannot negate your value. It is not material things that give you value; your value comes from knowing who you are and why you're here. You are a uniquely created being who was put on earth for a special purpose that you alone can fulfill. You will never compare yourself to anyone when you understand that. You are designed for a purpose, and your purpose was designed for you. No one can take your place or occupy your space in this world. You're an original—a masterpiece.

If you don't understand your uniqueness and value, you will always be a victim of other people's opinions. There are certain things I like to say to myself when I wake up in the mornings. I look at myself in the mirror and say, "You're a God-child. You're in the God-class. You're classy baby!" I base my worth on my relationship with my superior source—God. I am Him; He is me. He is perfect; therefore, I am perfect. My worth comes from He who lives within me and that's solid. Unshakeable. I give things value; things don't give me value.

As I close my narrative, I encourage you: never give away your personal power to anyone. Know yourself to know your worth and be strong and courageous.

Karlene Millwood is an award-winning author, screenwriter, playwright, speaker, and life strategist who is passionate about empowering others to live their best life. She has written two published books; written, produced and directed the 2014 play, *Forgiven;* and produced two short films, one of which she also wrote and directed.

Facebook: https://www.facebook.com/KAMMIntl

Twitter: http://www.twitter.com/SweetlyDvine

Instagram: http://www.instagram.com/karlenemillwood

Linkedin: https://www.linkedin.com/in/kmillwood/

My Life Change Was Inevitable

by Kathi A. Holliday

While playing volleyball at college, I started itching and swelling all over my body. I had no idea what was going on. Afraid, freaking out and crying, I drove myself home. Entering my home, I screamed, mom! My parents freaked out when they saw my face, arms and legs. As I was frantically telling them what happened, the itching and swelling was getting worse by the minute.

We immediately traveled to the doctor's office. After I had suffered for two-and-a-half hours (traveling and waiting for the doctor), the itching and swelling subsided. The doctor unequivocally said I had an allergic reaction—hives. I handled my allergies as best I could for a decade, but never did I think death would cross my door not once but twice in my lifetime.

At my ten-year class reunion, I missed dinner on purpose, but I did taste a piece of beef followed by dancing. Almost immediately I knew that was a big mistake. Leaving the reunion, I could barely breathe as I walked into the emergency room and then fainted. Awakened in tears, I promised myself to do better.

Nine years later on a first date with a perfect gentleman, it happened again. I was so embarrassed. We dined at Red Lobster and danced afterwards, unaware that eating seafood would be a death sentence for me. Arriving home, I was weak, hot and very itchy. I thanked my date while exiting the car, but he insisted on walking me to my apartment door. Thank God he did, because I fainted thereafter. My glands swelled, making it very hard to breathe, and when the paramedics arrived, I had no pulse.

The dermatologist concluded after these two frightening occurrences that whenever I eat, I must relax six to eight hours before any strenuous exercise including dancing, roller skating or working out. I had to come to terms quickly, because this was a serious adjustment for me being very active and a food connoisseur. However, I am determined to survive and I tell myself daily that my life depends on this inevitable change. Literally!

Raised on the far South Side of Chicago, Illinois, Kathi Holliday received her bachelor's degree in business administration from Governors State University. She has successfully dominated the entrepreneurship world for fourteen years as chief executive officer of UFS (an organizational company), and Mobile Notary 24/7 in the state of Arizona.

Website: www.MobileNotary247.com
Podcast: www.TheMobileNotaryShow.podbean.com
Podcast: Anchor.fm/MobileNotary247
Facebook Page: www.facebook.com/KathiNotaryHolliday
Facebook Business Page: www.facebook.com/MobileNotary24Seven
Instagram Page: www.instagram.com/MobileNotary247
LinkedIn Page: www.LinkedIn.com/in/MN247
Twitter Page: www.twitter.com/MobileNotary24K

My Life as a Hamster

by Kathy Maloney

What does a hamster have to do with how I've been living my life for twenty-five years? It's simple: a hamster gets on a wheel and she runs. She runs faster and faster but isn't going anywhere. That was me in a nutshell: I was and still am very busy. The difference is that today I am getting off the hamster wheel. I have figured out where I am running to and it feels liberating and exciting.

For years I tried to figure out what my contribution to the world is. How could I make money doing something I loved? The answer was never clear to me until my cousin asked me a very simple question: what matters to you? I really thought about it. I've always helped and encouraged others to be better at what they had planned for their lives. Meanwhile, my wheel kept spinning. I went from being a social service worker to running a public relations business; to becoming an actor and an acting coach; to running a cleaning service; to selling second-hand clothing; to event planning and finally, to becoming a certified travel agent.

What really matters to me is helping family, friends, colleagues, and even strangers feel confident within themselves; and helping them accomplish their goals any way I can. I am a performer with an entrepreneurial spirit who is ready to get off the hamster wheel. I've created a podcast called Life Stripes with Kathy and Duke, launching in the Spring of 2019. We will focus on conversations about relationships, life, career, and anything else that helps our listeners grow in their personal journey. We will cater to Generation X and anyone else who wants to join us.

Yes, our lives get messy and chaotic behind the scenes, but when the curtain opens it's time to reveal our true selves unapologetically. I challenge you to jump off the hamster wheel and run into the life you are meant to live.

 Kathy Maloney is an energetic mom of two, as well as an actor and an acting coach. She co-hosts the podcast, Life Stripes with Kathy and Duke to share her positive spirit and fuel her desire to learn from and help others problem solve through this event called life.

https://www.instagram.com/officialkathymaloney/

Success Despite the Fear

by Kim Thompson-Pinder

I spent my childhood full of fear and afraid to be who I truly was. An event when I was seven cemented that belief that I was not worthy.

My mother died when I was four, so my female grade-two teacher became a substitute mom. I loved to write stories and every day I would proudly hand them to my teacher, waiting for her praise. At first, she was interested, but months of this wore her down.

One day she said, "Kim you're not good at writing, please stop doing it." I was devastated. My creative soul was crushed, and except for school projects I did not write again for thirty-three years.

But…

In retrospect, I was an emotionally needy child. As I look at my teacher's picture, I realize she was young, not married, and childless. She was unprepared for my needs, so she did what she had to, and you know what?

I forgive her.

I've realized that I am responsible for my future. I could use her as an excuse, or I could let it go, and that is what I did.

When I was forty an opportunity came to write, and I had a decision to make: let what someone said thirty-three years before stop me or move forward. So, battling the fear, I wrote a blog post and shared it with others. People liked it, so I wrote more.

Eighteen months later, the box was gone, and my first book was started. It took a year, but I got it done. Within the next two years, another four were published, and I was earning some money from the sales.

Eighteen months after that I took another step forward and began ghostwriting books for professionals who couldn't write their own. For someone who didn't write for over thirty years, I now write thousands of words a day that help others.

Never let anyone stop you from becoming successful. If I can become a paid, professional writer at age forty, then there is nothing you can't do.

You are never too old to live your dream, and Kim Thompson-Pinder is proof of that. At age forty, she became an author, and now, six years later, she is the owner of a publishing company that helps others get their message out and become authors.

www.KimThompsonPinder.com

https://www.linkedin.com/in/wordninjakim/

https://www.facebook.com/groups/theauthorpreneurs/

The Other Side of the Badge

by Kimberly Mosby

My days are filled with researching and reading about the delicate psyches of us mere mortals. I search for answers to my own powerlessness, and to how to fulfill the purpose of my journey. I take stock of myself quite a bit. This self-evaluation comes at a time when I am approaching a milestone birthday and the completion of a long-term goal. These upcoming events force me to take a self-inventory.

My graduation from undergrad is right around the corner and I am filled with excitement and anticipation. This has been a journey that started right after high school. I sought my degree and played cat and mouse with it over the last forty years. On the way to this place and time in my life, even to my own surprise, I became a police officer, a member of Chicago's finest for twenty years. It was in my position in law enforcement that I came face-to-face with the mental health crisis that plagues American society today. I observed that the majority of repeat offenders, those people who came into contact with the police on a regular basis, were in need of mental health services.

My first-hand experience up close and in the trenches gave me the desire to "go on the other side of the badge" so to speak. The other side of the badge refers to becoming involved with prevention, with reaching people before they become actual criminals. This means that mental health services have to be implemented and offered on a wide-scale basis. Mental health centers can no longer be one center in a few areas of the city; these programs and centers have to flourish on almost every corner.

My major goal as a psychologist is to work towards bringing new and innovative ways to provide mental health services to these underserved areas. I dedicate my life not only to writing and researching programs that promote mental and emotional well-being, but also to bringing comprehensive mental health programs to schools, community centers, churches and the like. This will empower people to change the direction of their lives.

Kimberly Mosby, BA psychology, is a retired Chicago police officer with 20 years of service. She is also a member of Sisters on a Journey; African American Association of Black Psychologists; Hyde Park Community Players; and Sista Afya, Mental Wellness Group.

I Could Not Look into the Mirror

by Lalita Vaid

I remember waking up in the middle of the night almost all of my life screaming, "Help! Help!" and then finding myself alone and defenseless, drenched in fear. I thought I was the most normal human on this planet until one day I collapsed and woke up in an emergency ward alone, abandoned and engulfed in grief. The doctor told me point blank that I'd had a nervous breakdown.

My life was as dark as my nightmares. I sabotaged myself and broke my relationships. I looked for reasons to hibernate. I judged others and blamed them for my state of mind. Constant loss of love and bad relationships had hijacked my self-confidence, and I always felt low on energy, powerless and fearful. I had lost the rhythm of simple communication too, and developed a huge fear of public speaking. My self-esteem became so low that I stopped looking at myself in the mirror because I had developed body image issues. Financial growth and progress had given up on me long ago so it was not only loneliness I was dealing with; I was also broke. In spite of being in such a state, I thought that I was perfectly normal.

Then in 2007 my breakdown made me decide to take ownership of my power and walk onto a path of self-awareness. I went through self-awareness meditations and counseling to learn how to develop a relationship with myself so that I could develop good relationships with others. I also learned about my dark side and how to accept it, which helped me come out of loneliness and grief and maintain those relationships. I got in touch with my inner child, my anger and fear, and learned that I was the creator of all my circumstances. My nightmares disappeared. Understanding my fear helped me understand my power and strength to face my life obstacles with much clarity. It helped me take back my power and take ownership of my life.

It's important to plug in to who you really are to get connected to the world. Are you ready to plug in?

 Lalita Vaid is an author, entrepreneur, and teacher. She has helped many men and women to empower themselves by overcoming their fears and walking past their broken relationships with themselves and others so that they can live the lives of their dreams.

https://lalitavaid.com/

https://www.facebook.com/connectretreat/

https://www.facebook.com/lalitavaidpage

https://www.instagram.com/vaidlalita/

https://twitter.com/HolisticMist

https://www.linkedin.com/in/lalita-vaid-15489594/

Breaking Barriers, Finding Peace

by Laura Avolese

I see her when I close my eyes: Her smiling face, her soft touch, her warm embrace. This is what I see now, but it wasn't always this way.

There was a time when I closed my eyes and thought of her lying in a pool of her own blood, my mafioso father standing in the background. That vision haunted me. My mother's murder affected me for years in ways I didn't know or understand. One horribly violent act that gripped my entire family, that still has a hold on some of us.

But not me. Not now.

I learned to let go, to forgive.

Abuse in some form –physical, emotional, sexual–followed me in the wake of my mother's death. I turned to drugs to numb my pain. Young and pregnant, marriage was my only option according to my traditional Italian grandparents. Looking back, I wasn't ready and it brought me more abuse and pain. But, I've learned that from the worst pain comes the most incredible joy. For me, that joy is my two beautiful children.

When I think back to those days I often wonder where I found the courage to leave, to start again as a single mother with nothing and later, how I coped. The truth is I survived, but I wasn't living.

In 1995, I was so depressed that I had a major panic and anxiety attack. A close friend could see I needed help and enrolled me in a LifeStream course led by an extraordinary man named Jim Quinn.

Jim was instrumental in my healing, a healing that required me to forgive. With Jim's help, I forgave my father for the murder. And, years later, I forgave my mother for not being there for me as I grew up alone and abused.

I was drowning in anger and resentment. Forgiveness brought me peace, happiness, and success. Most surprisingly, forgiveness gave me purpose. Now, through speaking and my book, *Breaking Barriers* I help others rediscover their power and success by teaching them how to let go and forgive.

 Laura Avolese is a successful realtor, mother, and speaker. From childhood, Laura shouldered heavy burdens, and although she stumbled occasionally, she used her inner strength to reach new levels of success. Laura's incredible life story reveals how forgiveness, spirituality, and determination helped her forge a happy life and successful career.

Website: www.lauraavolese.com

Instagram: https://www.instagram.com/lauraavolese/

Contact: laura@lauraavolese.com

Facebook: http://fb.me/AvoleseLaura

Twitter: @Breakingb2017

Love is the Answer

by Lauren E. Jones

The Universe is brilliant and supportive, but she recently offered me a tough lesson: my boss sexually assaulted me.

The fear and shock was paralyzing. Fear has the ability to cause life to spin out of control. It can prevent growth, happiness and love. Fear, anger and shame are commonly felt emotions following trauma. One must feel and process these emotions; however, in order to heal, there must be a conscious effort to move away from fear-based thoughts towards love-based actions. Hanging on to anger will not change the past, but it will affect the present moment and the future.

Fear can only thrive if we feed it. Fear isn't real; it's something we create in our minds. The only thing that is real, from a spiritual perspective, is love. Choosing love over fear is not the typical instinctual reaction following sexual assault. However, I had a deep knowing in my soul that love was the answer to my healing. Everything happens for a reason and I was determined to accept my fate, understand the meaning and heal with love.

I healed in reliance on love-based spiritual principles and practices. Broadly speaking, I changed my perspective to one that was focused on love. I chose to see this harmful experience as a lesson wrapped up in a blessing. In order to truly love yourself and heal, you must accept the experiences that shaped you. You can't change what happened to you, but you can control whether you let yourself be reduced by it. There is always something to learn from our dark moments.

When the Universe smacks you down, it is teaching you a valuable lesson: to choose love. When you change your perspective, any circumstance can be perceived as meaningful. I found my life purpose; to help those who have suffered trauma heal through love-based practices. I offer my clients customized sessions to inspire and empower them to open up to love on their healing journey. I would be honored to guide you on your journey towards love.

Love is always the answer.

Lauren E. Jones is an author, spiritual teacher, meditation coach, and love warrior. She supports her clients to awaken, heal, and transform by relying on her spiritual knowledge, life experiences, and intuitive abilities. Lauren is currently writing *Love is the Answer* where she shares her healing journey following sexual assault.

www.laurenjones.ca

Learning to Slow

by Lauren Williamson

There's this humble and quiet part of me that knows I love crawling into bed with a warm cup of herbal tea, my dogs nestled beside me, and a book on whatever may be piquing my interest. There's nothing more soul nourishing. It's the feminine energy, beautiful and nurturing. It calms the storm and the rigid discipline of the masculine mind of my often dominant, type A personality. That energy can be all consuming and ultimately costly when it comes to the pursuit of what's truly best for the spirit. The feminine works to remind us of what the heart knows and the head needs.

I suppose this is where I've learned to find resilience in much of the adversity we experience in life. I've grown to understand that challenge tends to present itself at times when the heart and body are screaming to be heard. Times when the masculine mind has existed unbalanced in the driver's seat for too long. It's in these times that I typically find myself drawn back either to a yoga mat or to the ocean. For me, these places offer a refuge where the soul gets its time to chime in and do its thing, sorting the muddled mind out.

Often, it's in the most gentle child's pose that I experience a deep sense of strength—not a bodily one, but purely consciousness related and that's powerful. I find myself deeply humbled by all that I am doing, instead of what I think I should be doing.

So how is it that this practice of simply slowing fulfills my type A, need to achieve personality? It's because I've learned to allow it to be exactly what it's supposed to be. I've embraced and created a space for it; I've nurtured it when it needed coddling, welcomed and allowed the gifts it holds. This space has opened up an incredibly nurturing sense of strength and accomplishment no masculine energy has ever offered me. It's provided a deep gratitude for the blending of these polar forces within us all.

Lauren Williamson is an artist and writer whose inspiration is deeply rooted in her love for natural elements and personal exploration. Her home is the Pacific Northwest, a landscape that serves as yet another provoking muse.

www.lauren-williamson.com

info@lauren-williamson.com

Lots to Be Thankful For

by Lawrence Beesley

My grandfather was an atheist and survived the war. I experienced many hardships: my wife Diane and my mother dying; my sister Linda and myself battling mental illness; and my son, Christopher, battling asthma. By God's grace, my family and I became born again Christians. I am thankful to my wife Claudette; my son; his wife Angela; and my three grandchildren, Caesar, Cyrus, and Cassius.

When Lawrence Clifton Beesley was born, the umbilical cord was strangled around some vertebrae which fused two of them together, resulting in a birth defect. But Lawrence was a survivor. He even had a relative from England who survived the Titanic. Google the name Lawrence Beesley, and you'll be amazed.

Know Thyself

by Lee Davy

"Know thyself and thou shalt know the Universe and
God"
- Temple of Apollo

Go to school, get a job, work fifty years, vacation, retire, and if your health remains, enjoy your twilight years, then… die?

Whoa! What? It never resonated. My search began. I didn't realize it was a journey back to *knowing myself.*

Something happened many eons ago, a fall in consciousness—the "dark ages"—like a plague squashing our purity. We forgot, became trapped in *these* forms without knowing what we were. The year 2012 (perceived by some as the *end times*) began the age of Aquarius and a return to greater consciousness of who we really are— latent capabilities emerging.

It's an unprecedented time in history; with the world and systems around us crumbling.

Yet, there is the simultaneous emergence of organizations; the intersection of science and spirituality—new beliefs, proving that by focusing and honing our minds, we can change how we feel, and create a new reality (shifting from the Newtonian to quantum model).

After years of feeling alien, alone, and riddled with anxiety, with the above awarenesses I finally pieced together the puzzle of who I am, experiencing more oneness, knowing, and bliss as my journey continues.

A lifetime seeker and researcher, I've always questioned *reality*, daring exploration beyond the senses, mentoring with masters of our time, and piecing together this cosmic puzzle.

Before, I was never comfortable in my own skin. I first remember questioning at thirteen when I was told that church, school, and government had the answers.

They did, and do not.

Earth was constructed as a playground for the Universe to experience matter and beauty, learning and discovering in a manner which, without these forms isn't possible.

I've come to understand, believe, and *know*, that earth was created for me, by me, as a means to experience physicality.

Now, looking back with deepened understanding, and remembrance, I realize it's been a journey all along.

I am what I am. Purity. Love. Consciousness.

I am, *as are you*, the Universe, expressing itself in physical form for this brief period.

Lee Davy helps people piece together the puzzle of who they really are and what they're truly capable of, leveraging tools and perspectives (including movement, nutrition, science of mind and body, and energy work) gained from over three decades of contemplation, study, and assimilation of the consciousness and healing arts.

Website: https://lee-davy.com/

Facebook: https://www.facebook.com/lee.davy.507

LinkedIn: https://www.linkedin.com/in/lee-davy/

Instagram: https://www.instagram.com/transcend171/

Connecting the Dots

by Lee Davy

"You cannot connect the dots looking forward, you can only connect them looking backwards. Trust they align."
- Steve Jobs

I know now the dots were realigning me with my true self as I gained clarity, gathering tools as a seeker nearly my entire life. I know now it had always been a destined journey.

I realize now, my anxieties, 'alien' feelings, and discomfort in my own skin were the catalysts that led to my search and ultimate discovery of the quantum sciences, meditation practices, healing modalities, and understanding that my soul and persona "Lee" yearned for in this lifetime.

Something deep within as a child remembered, somehow, that I'd been here before—many lifetimes. As a result, perceptions garnered through my five senses held no truth, and a healing journey—the journey of a lifetime—ensued.

This is the journey, and these are the tools I now share with the world as we transition, cross paradigms from the old world into a new one.

Akin to Plato's allegory of the cave (the prisoner climbs out of the cave to discover the real world and wants so badly for fellow prisoners to *know truth),* we are leaving the cave, and entering the cosmic penthouse, if you will. We are literally awakening from dense matter to the conscious, light-beings we truly are.

With the use of a variety of tools and perspectives, I have finally pieced together the puzzle of who I truly am and what I'm capable of. The feelings of disconnection and unworthiness, and a body riddled with anxieties have long passed in favor of reconnecting with, and fully stepping into my power. Now I am using my voice, story, and the tools I've garnered during this journey to assist others in their own journey to fully understanding and embracing their highest selves.

Despite our programmed beliefs, truth is irrefutable to our souls. I trust you hear truth and it ignites or furthers your journey back to knowing yourself, and your true capabilities. If my story can bridge conscious awakening for even one other person, it is worth writing.

 Lee Davy helps people piece together the puzzle of who they really are and what they're truly capable of, leveraging tools and perspectives (including movement, nutrition, science of mind and body, and energy work) gained from over three decades of contemplation, study, and assimilation of the consciousness and healing arts.

Website: https://lee-davy.com/

Facebook: https://www.facebook.com/lee.davy.507

LinkedIn: https://www.linkedin.com/in/lee-davy/

Instagram: https://www.instagram.com/transcend171/

A Survivor's Mindset

by Lester Bailey

Mindset is the way you think about something or believe something to be. It is the one thing that separates you from being a victim of your circumstances or a survivor of them.

When I was a police officer, I used to drive up and down the streets and see people walking around aimlessly, not paying attention to their surroundings, or the people around them. They couldn't tell you what they were wearing, how tall or short they were, if they were black or white, whatever the race.

Most people are walking around with no direction. They tell themselves, "I'll never be the victim. I will never be that person anything ever happens to," *ou*, the Universe, expressing itself in but they don't understand that predators are watching them. They're standing in the shadows or in plain view. Your criminal doesn't have a certain look — tall, short, big, or small. Your criminal looks like deceit, desperation, cunning, even someone you know.

As a young police officer, I was the victim of a crime. I was walking down the beachfront, and three guys came out of nowhere and robbed me and my brother. It scared me something bad. But understanding that that event happened for that moment we continued on our way, thinking of how this would never happen to us again. We would learn to be more attentive to everything and everybody and then tell someone.

If you are a victim of a crime, it's not the end of all end games, but you must change your mindset. If you let a bad situation take you over, you become a victim every day. When you accept that the crime happened and continuously move on with life, you become a survivor, a strong survivor.

Lester Bailey, graduate of DePaul University, Chicago, is retired from the Chicago Police Department. He is a #1 international, best-selling author; motivational speaker; podcaster; and community organizer; involved with ministry and bodyguarding for a United States senator. Lester is a testament to diligence, dedication, determination, and service to others.

Podcast: https://nocn4u.podbean.com/

Relentless

by Lester Bailey

If anyone should ever ask about my life story, for whatever reason there might be, tell them I've had ups and downs. There were so many times I doubted myself. I had low self-esteem. No confi-dence. I believe that darkness followed me because there were so many times, so many things that did not go right. We have all been there a time or two. Right?

I remember there were times I went to work, hoping that they would promote me to a supervisor position. I worked my butt off for the promotion, only for it to be given to a friend of the boss. When I complained I got terminated from my position. During that time, I'd just had a newborn ba-by and bills were piling up fast. That was a dark time in my life.

I really began searching for a major change. I needed motivation. And then I got it—I went to moti-vational conferences and got inspired. They told me that if I wanted change in my life then I must be the change I wanted. So, I began reading motivational books and listening to tapes.

I stared to build my self-confidence. It was told to me, "If thoughts are things, what are you think-ing? Guard your thoughts." So, I wanted to become a police officer and help people, and I did.

Let me tell you now that all things can be yours if you can simply believe in yourself. Have faith, not fear. Faith and fear are the same things. Both are the unknown. Which one will you follow? I followed faith and thank God I did. So, here's my advice. Lead with character and be a person with integrity. Reshape your life, work on your mindset, follow your desires. Follow your dreams no matter how big, follow them wherever they may go. Make better decisions in your life. All you need is a plan, a roadmap, and the courage to press on. Be relentless.

Signed,

Love Yourself

Lester Bailey, graduate of DePaul University, Chicago, is retired from the Chicago Police Department. He is a #1 international, best-selling author; motivational speaker; podcaster; and community organizer; involved with ministry and bodyguarding for a United States senator. Lester is a testament to diligence, dedication, determination, and service to others.

Podcast: https://nocn4u.podbean.com/

Who Am I?

by Liliana Guadagnoli

Who Am I?

I am your big sister and soul sister that you come to for comfort, warmth and guidance. I am the one who holds all your secrets in my heart. I am the sister that you confide in about your girlfriend or boyfriend. I am the sister that you share your life with, and no one else knows. I am the sister whose shoulder you cry on. I am the sister who laughs hysterically with you.

Who Am I?

I am your lover, to embrace and be embraced with love and affection, to be one with you. I am your lover to forever hold you, oh so tightly, and to love you unconditionally for eternity. If you were to choose a color for our love, what would it be? Red, green, yellow, white, purple, pink? You choose. If it has a shape, what shape would it be—round, triangle, diamond, or star? If it has a texture, what texture would it be—smooth, rough, pointy, soft, or jelly like? What temperature would it be? Now, with your hands take what you just created as a symbol of love and place it in your heart. It is now in the chambers of your heart and pulsating, thump-thump, thump-thump, thump-thump! Feel it, breathe it, live it. I am with you for eternity. Thump-thump.

Who Am I?

I am your mother, who gave you birth and witnessed the miracle of life. I am your mother who wiped your baby tears, who made you smile, who made you laugh. I am your mother who taught you to walk, who protected you from every fall. I am your mother, who did homework with you; and who took you to skating, swimming, soccer, and baseball. I am your mother who consoled you as a teenager, who gave you my car so you could have fun with your friends, and who was up all night waiting until you came home safely. Now you have moved out and started a life with your soul mate, and I will always be your loving mother.

Liliana Guadagnoli is an intuitive healer, Reiki Master, spiritual coach, #1 international best- selling author, and poet. Her devotion to helping others connect to their inner power is why she is committing her life in service of spiritual enlightenment. Her own miracles of healing have now become her purpose.

https://www.facebook.com/liliana.guadagnoli

www.soulnatomy.com

Who Am I?

by Liliana Guadagnoli

Who Am I?

I am your aunt, who takes care of you when your parents go to work. I am the crazy aunt who buys you gifts that put a smile on your face. I am the aunt you tell secrets to about why your mom and dad won't let you do the things you want to do. I am the aunt that gives you my car to drive your friends to the corner store. I am your favorite aunt and I know you love me too.

Who Am I?

I am your grandmother, who smothers you with kisses every time I see you. I am your grandmother who guides you in your journey of life and protects you from those crazy friends of yours. I am your grandmother, who uplifts you when you are down, who empowers you to be the best that you can possibly be. I am your grandmother who secretly takes you to places that mommy and daddy won't and buys you everything you want. I am your grandmother, whose cell phone you secretly snatched, right under my nose when I was napping, then took a picture of me and sent it to my friends. I am your embarrassed grandmother, and I love you.

Who Am I?

I am your best friend and your confidante. I am all of the above: sister, soul sister, lover, mother, aunt, and grandmother. What is there left to say? You make me whole and complete. You make me who I am today. It is because of you that I am able to help others; it is because of you that I have the gift of healing others; and it is because of you that I can *love* without fear. It is you that I am thankful for and it is God that I am thankful for who brought us together.

I am your everlasting friend for eternity.

Liliana Guadagnoli is an intuitive healer, Reiki Master, spiritual coach, #1 international best- selling author, and poet. Her devotion to helping others connect to their inner power is why she is committing her life in service of spiritual enlightenment. Her own miracles of healing have now become her purpose.

https://www.facebook.com/liliana.guadagnoli

www.soulnatomy.com

Think Your Way to Success

by Linda Procopio

I learned over the years that our thoughts are very powerful and only we can stand in our way of fulfilling every desire. When you truly desire to change, it will magically happen since the universe has your back.

Try to identify what you want to achieve, develop an action plan, and go for it! Being fearful, while totally normal and natural can be extremely frustrating. It can hinder your ability to enjoy experiences or stop you from taking risks. Fear comes from visualizing the negative outcomes. Try visualizing the outcome that favors you most. You will reach your goal a lot easier if you are feeling happy and confident.

The most important thing in life is you. A healthy, loved, happy, fearless, and determined you. Our health is determined by our thoughts, nutrition and environment. If we don't have our health, we have nothing!

I challenge you to become aware of your thoughts and think only positive for an entire day. Being aware of it is the first step. Once you realize that, it will be easier to replace your negative thoughts with positive thoughts. Take it one step further and try communicating only positive words for twenty-four hours. Also, listen to those around you since you will start to notice that most people are very negative. If you find this activity challenging at first, don't give up. All you need is faith!

I was able to overcome many challenges through determination, desire and faith. I decided to start my own business as a holistic nutrition expert after losing my father to cancer. I am determined to help as many people as I can to prevent and overcome diseases such as diabetes, high blood pressure, thyroid, liver, kidney disorders, insomnia and so much more. I help men and women around the world achieve greatness by teaching them how to change their thoughts, eat the foods that are right for their body, drink the best water for pure hydration, and breathe the cleanest air. These four elements are the key secrets to living a vital, happy, healthy life!

 Linda inspires others to take control of their health, transform their bodies, and change their lives. She's at the forefront of exciting, proactive approaches to health; and is a certified metabolic balance coach; chef; and an author of *Empowering Women to Succeed*. She coaches those wanting to reverse health challenges.

Websites: www.livelitebylinda.ca

www.metabolic-balance.com/ca

Facebook: https://www.facebook.com/livelitebylinda/

Instagram: https://www.instagram.com/livelitebylinda/

Passion to Purpose

by Linsey Fischer

I always knew I wanted to be a writer. When I was a little girl, I used to sit on my windowsill, writing in my diary. I felt so at peace in those moments. Writing was always a part of me because it was something I enjoyed. It brought me great comfort, and a way to express all of my emotions. It was mind, to pen, to paper.

Through the years, I accomplished a lot with my writing abilities. I wrote a weekly column in my hometown newspaper and gained experience in broadcast journalism, where I wrote my own broadcasting scripts and news stories. While the opportunities were great, the money was not there. It was a struggle to make a living from my passion, so I stepped away from the industry to go after jobs that were going to pay me what I needed to survive.

Throughout my mid-twenties, I was all over the place. Although I started to make some money, I didn't feel fulfilled. A nine-to-five life felt like a life sentence rather than a life of purpose. Your typical millennial, I was stubborn, refusing to give up on my dream. It was time to give it another try.

I did some major soul-searching and decided to make a real effort to use the resources available to me in the community. I went to job fairs and networking events, and I volunteered. Through this, I discovered entrepreneurship and met people in the book industry.

At twenty-seven, I started at the bottom and worked my way up in the writing world. It didn't feel like work; it was pure joy. By twenty-nine, I became a three-time, best-selling author and edited two best-selling books. Now, at thirty years old, I'm the senior editor of the next book in the *Empowering Women to Succeed* series and an author coach. I am making money, and I turned my passion into purpose.

I always knew I wanted to be a writer, so I made it my mission. If you put in the work, you can accomplish anything you want to.

 Linsey Fischer is a four-time #1 international best-selling author, editor, and writing coach. She is also an award winner for her work on the *Empowering Women to Succeed* book series; a contributing author to the books, *365 Life Shifts* and *Goodness Abounds*; and a former newspaper columnist and broadcast journalist.

LinkedIn: https://ca.linkedin.com/in/linsey-fischer-7a3475b0

Facebook: https://m.facebook.com/linsey100/?ref=bookmarks

Driven: The Untold Story Behind My Success

by Lisa da Rocha

People that know old Lisa would say that I am driven, accomplished, and successful. They may share that my partner and I co-founded and grew a multi-million-dollar business, and that I had a successful corporate career having been the youngest executive in several companies and appointed to the top one percent of employees worldwide by a global organization. They may also share that I own rental properties, volunteer, and have three small children and a loving marriage with my high school sweetheart. They would describe me as driven. This was the Lisa that most people met, the Lisa that played the role of high-powered executive by day and supermom by night.

What I'd like to share with you today is the behind-the-scenes Lisa, the Lisa that most people didn't see and—the untold story behind my success.

The truth is, while I had success the old Lisa gained it at a cost. A big cost to my happiness, health and relationships. My drive for success came from fear, a hunger to prove, and a need for recognition. I wanted accolades, acknowledgment—applause even! No matter what I accomplished, it was never good enough because I was in it for the wrong reasons; I attached my self-worth to achievements and so when I wasn't stretching myself to the brink of exhaustion, it simply wasn't sufficient.

And then it changed. I turned forty, we welcomed baby number three, and my work felt undemanding. I became depressed, I questioned everything, and things seemed to fall apart around me. It was a tough time and yet, I am eternally grateful for it. Through the process of sitting in the mess, evaluating my life, examining what was truly important, and ultimately understanding the unhealthy nature of the fuel that drove me, I was able to gain a new perspective.

Today, I am still driven. My drive, however, is fueled by a desire to contribute, not a need to feed my ego. I accomplish in service of others and to make a positive impact. I live. I learn. I serve. And yes, I still succeed.

Lisa da Rocha co-founded a multi-million-dollar company in her twenties. Later, as a corporate executive, she was ranked in the top 1 percent of leaders worldwide. Currently, she is a highly sought-after executive coach. She is most proud of her three children and fifteen-year marriage to her high school sweetheart.

www.lisadarocha.com

Light

by Lisa Buhrow

I could hear sirens in the distance. As I opened my eyes, I saw bright, white light and I felt a hand wiping glass from my eyes. A voice said, "Lisa, I am here, and you are going to be ok." By the time I was checked in to the emergency room it was clear that I had been in an accident. I was hit on the driver's side by a full-sized van. My father took pictures of the car and kept telling me it was a miracle that I only had a seat belt burn and a few cuts on my face.

That was not to be the first time that I would need the assistance of angels.

When I started my business, one of my first clients, John, had been in a serious motorcycle accident. He had pins, steel rods, and plates in his legs.

As I began massaging him, I could feel the pain in his body and I thought, I'm not sure I can do this, I don't know if I am capable enough. The self-doubt was overwhelming, I felt like I was drowning, and then there it was—a bright white light. I knew then that all I had to do was pray and ask for help.

When the massage was over, John said he felt better, but within the next twenty-four hours I received an urgent phone call from him, saying he had to see me immediately.

I met him at the door to my business asking, "Is everything ok? Are you in pain?"

He replied, "Lisa, I want to know exactly what you did yesterday."

I looked at him, contemplating how to be professional and if I should tell him how I prayed over him. Then I took a deep breath and a leap of faith. "I prayed for you, I asked the angels to take your pain away," I said.

He looked at me, and then he smiled and laughed, "That's wonderful, please do that again. That's the first time in ten years I haven't had pain."

Lisa Buhrow, a Reiki Master and instructor, has worked in the healing arts profession for twenty-two years. Her passion is people, and her deepest intention is to help others discover their natural healing abilities through Reiki and medical Qi Gong. Lisa is also a registered acupuncturist with Aboriginal Acupuncture, NS.

https://youtu.be/I5GEK7FxVDw

https://www.instagram.com/heavenlyqilisabuhrow/

heavenlyqilisabuhrow@gmail.com

Create a Life You Love

by Lisa Petsinis

I grew up thinking I would embark on a stable career in a helping profession, such as teaching. By chance, I landed in human resources work, progressed through the ranks, gained credentials and applied insight and empathy. I put my heart, soul, blood, sweat, and tears into my work.

Fast forward twenty years and my daughter looked up at me and asked if I was ever going to put my laptop away. It stung. There I was a single mom, trying to do it all with an over-stacked deck. Yes, I had a successful career, but the personal cost was too high. I was tired, stuck and empty, and my daughter wasn't getting the best of me.

The futility of the rat race hit me again when I was recovering from a health issue, lying in bed, contemplating my life: "How did I get here?" It was then that I chose to take responsibility for my future. I explored mindfulness and learned how to trust my intuition. I spent quality time with my beautiful, free-spirited daughter. I also hired a coach to explore my purpose. And I found it. I found me. I never felt more whole as the day I wrote my life script and visualized my life in perfect detail.

Then, with my vision imprinted in my mind, and in the face of naysayers, I realized the risk was only in my imagination. I gave myself permission to take a leap of faith. I left the corporate world, became a certified coach, built a business from scratch, became a syndicated writer, and integrated things I had previously sidelined like relationships and self-care.

My life completely changed. I felt alive and empowered. Now it's my mission to work with others who want to uncover their brilliance and bring their best selves to the world, too. When you do what you love, you shine.

Figure out what lights you up. You'll never regret following your heart and finding your calling. Even if you think the odds are against you, anything is possible. Start now and create a life you love.

Lisa Petsinis, ACC, CHRL, CDCS, is a certified career and life coach, who works with resourceful women who want to bring their best selves to their work and life. She's on a mission to create more confidence and joy, and her work has appeared in MSN, Prevention, POPSUGAR, and YourTango.

Website – https://www.lisapetsinis.com/

LinkedIn – https://www.linkedin.com/in/lisapetsinis/

Instagram – https://www.instagram.com/lisapetsiniscoaching/

Facebook – https://www.facebook.com/LisaPetsinisCoaching/

Pinterest – https://www.pinterest.ca/lisapetsinis/

Twitter – http://twitter.com/LisaPetsinis

Shifting from Shame to Self-Love

by Lisa Taraba

"You can't come into the classroom
until you say my name."
"Your name is teacher."
"No, what is my proper name?"

I froze with shame. I was unable to pronounce her name. While my first-grade teacher's question initiated my speech therapy, it also crushed a part of me. It taught me the fear of not being good enough. As life continued, experiences reinforced a belief that my worth was tied to validation from others. Yet, they also fuelled my desire for personal growth.

The birth of my first child was another opportunity to expand my perception of self-worth. As a teen, I learned that polycystic ovarian syndrome could prevent me from having children. As an adult, I shed many tears judging myself as incomplete. So, when my husband and I became parents, we knew we were blessed.

My faith in religion, however, was shattered when the Catholic Church deemed me morally wrong for being artificially inseminated by my husband. Our son was a gift! How was I morally wrong for taking medication to assist my ovaries? How was it different from taking medication to assist any other body part? I felt disillusioned and persecuted. I oscillated between sadness and anger. Attending church only brought tears. I grieved the loss of a religion that taught me spirituality, faith and love, because I could no longer ignore its fear-based teachings of judgment, shame and guilt.

Today, I am grateful for feeling condemned by the Church. The experience allowed me to connect with the depth of my internal strength and worth. I learned to love myself for the imperfections that make me who I am—a unique expression of Divine love. My name is Lisa and my two children are blessings. They woke my forgotten spiritual gifts and remind me of the magic of giving and receiving love. I now know that my spirituality is not bound to an institution, but to the endless flow of loving, universal energy that guides my moral compass and connects me to a world of joy, gratitude, and non-judgment.

Lisa Taraba, associate certified coach and founder of I Thrive Coaching, is passionate about inspiring people to find the power of their personal leadership. She helps clients rediscover their inspiration and purpose so they can become the fearless leaders they truly are and create the lives and businesses they desire.

https://ithrivecoaching.ca

Living Without Limits

by Liz Streich

From an early age, we believe what our parents, friends and family tell us: you can't do this, you can't do that. Then we hear our parents talk about getting older and not being able to do things because they are too old. "You can't teach an old dog new tricks" was the mantra. "I'm too old to do that now" is what we learned. These messages become so ingrained in us that they form part of our belief systems.

In January of 2015 I was sitting on my couch, staring out toward the trees, and reflecting on my life. I was fifty-seven. I knew that I had a youthful mind and yet my body felt old. I was overweight, out of shape, and in tremendous mental and physical pain. I started to ask myself questions about my future, but I thought I was too old to make changes. This limiting belief was an echo of what I heard my parents say as I was growing up. Deep down I knew somehow it did not feel right, and I began making changes.

I began chipping away at the limiting beliefs. I lost sixty pounds and developed muscle definition by managing my food intake, joining a gym and hiring a personal trainer. I also devoured personal development books. Gradually my confidence soared, and now I plan to share my journey through coaching, book writing and speaking.

There are three things you can do to change your life. First, decide how you want to live your life by dreaming about what you want to do. Once you realize what you want, you'll become happier because your values will be in alignment with who you are and what you truly desire.

Next, make a commitment to change. For me, that meant eating healthy and beginning an exercise program. For you it could be photography, reading poetry, or exploring painting. The possibilities are endless.

Finally, once you begin getting results, you will feel young again and start living the life you want. Join me on a journey to a youthful life!

 If anyone knows about a journey to a youthful life, it's Liz Streich. Liz was sick and tired of feeling exhausted, obese, old, and out of shape. So, she did something about it. She lost eighty pounds, got fit and now she inspires other people to live well.

https://lizstreich.com/

An Error of Judgment

by Lou Anne Reddon

"I'm scared," he whispered. "Hold my hand?" Then he was gone, leaving my hand empty, my heart full, and my life, both.

One dreary midwinter evening, Curt shuffled into the room where our public speaking club met and plunked down beside me. We all sidled away from the reek of smoke and stale booze.

He had stringy, long gray hair. Tattered jeans. Pearl Jam t-shirt. He slurred his words. We all thought he was looking for a rehab meeting, but every week, he'd show up.

I volunteered to mentor him. Our first session, Curt staggered into the appointed café, looked wildly around and stuttered, "I-I-I can't s-s-stay here. L-l-let's go b-b-back to my place."

My very first thought was, "Wow! You have a place?" I imagined he might live in a cardboard box downtown.

Dilemma. Should I follow a stranger home? He was so fragile and unsteady that I could have knocked him over easily, but what if he shared a crack house with some bikers? Oh c'mon, Lou, show some faith.

He led me to an upscale neighbourhood. Settling into his beautiful kitchen, he shared his story.

His daughter was getting married and he had joined our club to help him toast the bride. Then he confided that he suffered with multiple sclerosis. That's why he shuffled and was too shaky to shave.

I felt so ashamed for having misjudged this funny, fascinating character. Curt quickly became a much-loved member of our club, surprising us in his wedding tux the night of his toast's dress rehearsal. He rocked it on his daughter's wedding day! She burst into tears when she realized the tremendous effort her dad had made, just for her.

Eventually, Curt was confined to a wheelchair. We'd go for long walks along the river. He said, "I would have died long ago, if not for our club. Thanks for having taught me so much."

Oh, Curt, your lesson to me was so much greater—one I'll never forget until that day when I whisper for someone to hold my hand, too.

Based on her decades of professional copywriting experience, Lou Anne Reddon helps companies humanize B2B communications and strengthen emotional bonds with consumers. She's currently working on a book about the Underground Railroad in her native Niagara area, as well as a cookbook for men who are clueless in the kitchen.

www.lareddon.com

Blending in a Heartfelt Song: Colour, Voice, Light in a Dull and Noisy World

by Lynette Evans

It's one of those mornings again: two half-lidded, puffy eyes staring back at me. Mirrored. Reflecting. In this moment, I sort through what cannot be seen, hearing echoes long past, reciting all that could've or should've been. No answers, just swirling confusion and tears streaming forth.

I return to myself. "Do not. I repeat, do not retreat. Do not go back to bed!"

Ah, I've shifted into fighting mode again, morphed to assume the warrior's stance, opposing dark times spent curled up in a dull and noisy world.

Success? The idea flickered tangible once, but stretched beyond reach until my inner drill sergeant pushed through, relentless. His do-or-die posture, dare I admit, kept me going. But frontlines and trenches are not happy places to live; one void replaced another and I emerged more lost than found.

Who was I to assume perfection means loss—denying emotions? Feelings are real! Being human means moving forward, unraveling that illusion. When faced with challenge, what we do matters. How do we rise and break through?

Music answered first bearing aha moments, unexpected gifts, and seeding sound, silence, rhythm, breath, resonance, and tone. In a workshop we were shown how to sew frame drums and…click…I already knew what to do! My body hummed. I drummed. Strange… A knowing comfort settled in, meandering beyond the rational to transcend time and space.

Now, I flow with intention and purpose, expanding in breadth and depth—gathering up speed. Music invites access: new facets, dimensions, and versions of me I had never foreseen. And after twelve years as a singer in a choral, celestial, tour de force, I've found my ground, and stand firm and anchored. I ask my voice, my being, to beam resonant healing rays, expressing love above all. The more I reach out, the more I receive; the more I reach in, the more there is of me.

As I breathe into life, life breathes into me, gradual mastery.

My advice? Settle. Tune in. Stretch. Keep your body-instrument tall. Catch the upbeat, strike your chord, feel rhythm, be true, and above all, share your song.

Lynette Evans is a rare transformation coach. Valued by professionals, grounded in wisdom, she takes you into invisible areas: dissolving limitations and bringing you out better able to handle whatever you're going through. Integrating heart, mind, and spirit with leading-edge science, Lynette eases you towards alignment with passion and purpose.

www.HeartLightGrace.com

A New Life

By Lynn McIntosh

You never know what life has in store for you. Loss was my middle name ten years ago—loss and devastation beyond belief.

I married late thinking that since I had experienced life, had gained independence and had enjoyed the fun, single life my marriage would be solid and would last forever. I found out it's not the age at which you marry but the person you marry. I found out after a few years that I had married the wrong person for me. After ten years of marriage and struggles, I was divorced.

It was now a journey to find my inner strength for my children, and to stay on track. With the help and support of family and friends, I was able to do that.

Two years later my father passed away. Four months after his death I fell into a depression. I felt like a lost child, walking through the dark, literally. I would ask myself, "Why go on, why bother?" I would wonder, "I try so hard at life, but nothing works out. Why me?" There were days I would feel I could never make it to the evening. It felt like my soul had been ripped out.

Then I had an amazing experience that opened up my eyes. I started to look at what I had, not at what I didn't have. I would practice gratitude every day and give food and clothing to those who needed it. It took a huge amount of strength and courage to change. Some days it felt like I was ripping my outer layer of skin off, but step by step I did it.

Now I have created a new life for myself. It is an ongoing journey but every few months I come to a higher plateau and I know I could never go back to ten years ago. I just keep climbing that hill, for at the top is the reward of knowing I tried my best.

Never give up. Find your courage and strength.

Lynn McIntosh helps divorced women regain their confidence and thrive after leaving toxic relationships. Through coaching programs, clients release negative emotions, anger, sadness, frustration, and loneliness and regain their confidence and self-worth so they can move forward into living a joyful life. Lyn is a certified coach with GoPro Coaching.

www.lynnmcintosh.isagenix.com

Look at Me Now

by Maria Chiarlitti

Dear Past Self,

I've seen you torn down, shamed, lied to, and taken apart, while putting yourself back together.

Hurts a person should not have to endure, you endured, and no one was the wiser. You've risen above it and gathered up all the pieces of yourself spread over your timeline. You healed yourself because you knew it was your responsibility—yours and yours alone. Staying in the role of "victim" would do nothing for you, only drag you down further.

I've heard people say, we would have done things differently to protect ourselves if we'd only known. I don't see it that way. I accept what I went through, and it has made me who I am today. I'm in a place where I can breathe, live in joy, and be present in the moment. Each day painful memories wash away. They simply become a reminder that I have to put me first so that I can be the best that I can be, for my children, for myself, and so that I can help others live their optimal lives.

The peace I feel is incredible, the control over my own life empowers me, and this filters down to my children, teaching them that they are the ones responsible for how they handle situations in their lives. No matter how tough life can be sometimes, we must find ways to overcome the challenges, and live more in the light and less in the dark.

Past Self, I have so much gratitude in my heart for your strength, courage, and perseverance. I'm grateful for what you've taught me, helping me to become the human being I am today. I am able to honour myself, live in the present, and take action to live the life that I want to live.

I can finally look in the mirror, smile and say, look at me now!

Maria's passion and journey includes helping, healing, and empowering others on their journey so they can have extraordinary love and happiness. She is a Reiki master/teacher practitioner; a Quantum Healing Hypnosis Technique Practitioner; Crystal Reiki and Rainbow Reiki master/teacher practitioner; Akashic Records reader; and has her Medical Qigong Level III certification. Maria also owns MC Events.

Instagram: https://www.instagram.com/I_love_alberta/

Instagram: https://www.instagram.com/Mceventsbymaria/

Instagram: https://www.instagram.com/Joyoussoul888/

Website: https://www.mcevents.org/

Website: http://maria-grace.com

Winter Rose

by Marla David

You may think I am not here, but I am. I may have a disease, but I am still here. I may not remember everything—perhaps even you—and may have some trouble speaking and getting around, but the person you knew is still inside me. I have the same heart, and it beats to keep me alive. I have the same capacity to love, but you just can't see it.

Why is it that when people hear of my disease, they think I am not the person I was? I still laugh, feel emotion, and enjoy special moments. I intend on doing this as long as I can. There may be a day when I don't, but that doesn't change who I am at my essence. I know there are people who are my family, and I don't love them any less today than I did way back when.

If I could turn the clock back so I would be the person you want me to be, I would. By doing that though, I would be robbing you of this new story, which is tantamount to my dis-ease. You will always remember what you will about me, as everyone holds true their own memories.

Never in a million years did I ever see my future playing out this way. I'm not looking for your pity, nor do I want you to think of me as being weak. This is merely part of my journey in this life. Although this dis-ease continues to hold my mind and me hostage, I accept it. It doesn't sadden me because there is some reason I am walking this path, and I know in the bigger scheme of things, it plays a part in the history of our shared human story.

I don't know where the future will take me, but I am not afraid. I want you to know that. You need to know that I am okay, and I am still here. Things may have changed in my present circumstances, but heck—you still know me. I am still Rose.

Love, Rose

 Marla David is a life coach; speaker; writer; author of two #1 international bestsellers; and a retired stay-at-home mom with three grown daughters. She lives a life of passion, spending time with family and friends; traveling; enjoying arts and culture; advocating for animals and nature and giving back to society.

http://petluv1.wix.com/rosesandrainbows

Let it Be—
Designing a Life Toward Peace

by Marla David

I feel serene and at peace, allowing this sensation to fill and fulfill me like an inner glow or warmth. I float atop the water, as a leaf, effortlessly, pulled gently away from where I began, yet there is an all-knowing that I am headed to the source of all that is. I am calm.

Ding! The chime goes off and my meditation has ended. I come back to my awareness in the moment, relaxed and at ease.

"Row, row, row your boat, gently down the stream

Merrily, merrily, merrily, merrily, life is but a dream."

– Unknown

Stressing how imperative it is to have a positive outlook on life, this children's nursery rhyme says gently, not roughly. The less oppositional I am—detaching from the outcome and having faith that the Universe has my back—the simpler my life is. This lessens the struggle and constant worry, and I'm better able to float gently down the stream. By setting healthy boundaries, being responsible for my own life, I row my own boat too (something we all need to do). This allows me to be a better version of myself, and to show up for others in need.

When I go with the flow, just let it be, don't resist and allow life to unfold, things are easier and more peaceful. I'm not interfering, I let life just happen to me while I sit by and watch. There are also times when I need or choose to take the bull by the horns, especially if I can skirt any unnecessary stress.

Daily planning and goal-setting keep me in a state of flow and at ease, while I strive to reach my potential. I design my life around this concept. This goes a long way to enhancing the quality of my life, and I can go merrily down the stream, and just be happy.

"Now listen to what I said, in your life expect some trouble

When you worry you make it double

But don't worry, be happy, be happy now."

–"Don't Worry, Be Happy," by Bobby McFerrin

 Marla David is a life coach; speaker; writer; author of two #1 international bestsellers; and a retired stay-at-home mom with three grown daughters. She lives a life of passion, spending time with family and friends; traveling; enjoying arts and culture; advocating for animals and nature and giving back to society.

http://petluv1.wix.com/rosesandrainbows

A Personal Journey of Transformation — Learning to Be Me

By *Marlina Oliveira*

My journey to return to myself began five years ago with the passing of my mother. Watching her die a slow death was heart wrenching; her once vibrant mind and body dimmed and wilted away yet her soul, once buried deep within her, was emerging as the bright light she once was. When they say that there is life in dying, I believe that my mother's dying was a mirror for what had been dying within me; it was a chance to let go of what no longer served me and rise to who I was meant to be. Her death gave me life.

Grief gives you a path to a deep spirituality, and over the past few years, the old me began to unravel. My ego fought hard to keep me where I was—in pain, suffering, and fear—but this persona did not fit my soul. There was a continuous struggle between the external world and my inner world of knowing. The best of me, or what I believed was the best of me, had gone and I was left with someone I didn't know or like very much. I thought I would win this battle, but exhaustion prevailed and I knew I had to surrender.

As I write this, I am a month into letting go of the old layers, and healing. I am like a newborn baby trying to find its way in the world. I am deepening into my vulnerability, and seeking courage daily to feel the pain and to see my dark shadows rear their faces. The dark is my teacher. I have learned that you must face and embrace your dark side in order to step into the light. It is in this time that you become whole.

"And the day came when the risk to remain tight in a bud became more painful than the risk it took to blossom." Anaïs Nin

Marlina is a visionary who is inspired by innovative ideas. She has spent her life in the field of education, where her passion and ability to see the potential of each child motivated her to create her own elementary school. She is dedicated to supporting others in living their truth.

www.richlandacademy.ca

Pretending to Live

By Maxine Blagrove

I lived my life pretending everything was perfect; I played the role of a life that wasn't me. I was in complete denial that I was afraid of being rejected.

The temperature on my dashboard read minus 15 degrees—a typical January in Toronto. I still recall how feeble my foot was on the gas pedal and how my hands trembled on the steering wheel. They all wanted to let go, although I was still going at a high rate of speed. As more tears welled up, my breathing became erratic and my body started to tremble. Panic attack? No way, I thought, but it was too late. Oh my God, I'm having a panic attack! Without warning, I lost my sense of reasoning. I suddenly loathed myself. Disappointment set in and swiftly the need to let go and end it all felt more welcoming than trying to overcome it. I was in a dark place. I realized that I had been living my life with a desire to please people and my life was falling apart, because those same people were the ones who had rejected me.

That highway incident was several years ago and thankfully, I made it home safe. However, it took a lot of sacrificing and extreme self-care to get where I am today. I'll take you back to my childhood. All my life I'd been a "good girl," and I was taught to be kind and to stay out of trouble. I grew to be afraid of conflict and was petrified of speaking my mind. I ended up developing a low self-image with a deep desire to be accepted.

That panic attack was a fear of getting older and not being able to enjoy life. I realized that in order for me to become who I really was, I had to forgive myself, move out of my own way, and step into my purpose.

Today, I celebrate my authenticity by helping women to live life with clarity and purpose, and make good choices to maintain a healthy and happy lifestyle.

 Maxine Blagrove works with individuals who are ready to adopt and maintain a positive mindset towards life and their overall health and well-being. She believes it starts by removing the excuses and breaking the chains of negativity and self-doubt and realizing their true potential to live a more fulfilling life.

http://www.livewellwithmaxine.com

Let the Universe Lead You

by Maya Peron

After I got divorced, I met a man and after five years I moved with him and my youngest daughter to Canada. The love story did not go well and after a few months, my daughter and I were left alone—far from home, with poor knowledge of English, and without friends, working visas, or money. I was desperate, and at one point I was thinking of taking my own life.

Then I started meditating and actively using Attraction Symbols. It was not even a month later when an acquaintance called and asked if I could help his friend with something. I knew how hard it was when you are alone in a foreign country, so I gladly helped. We became good friends and I showed him the amulets we produced, and I gave him the only one I had with me at the time—Amar Nat, for love. He gave me a smile, and in return, I received a perfume with pheromones (attraction hormone) that he produced.

We laughed at the symbolism and quickly realized that we could also do business together—and do something good for the World and the people in it. After a few months, a new line of male and female perfumes was created, which, in addition to pheromones and liquid diamonds, are enriched by the high energy vibration of various Attraction Symbols.

Over time, I found out that it is necessary first to love and care for yourself, and then everything else will come together! Perhaps it was because of the amulet for Amar Nat? Perhaps it was because of the perfume I gladly used. Maybe because of both—or neither. Everything is energy and energy is everything. Sometimes you just need to step up! Today, not tomorrow. It was too much tomorrow already!

Maya Peron is a best-selling author; life coach; speaker; CEO of Attraction Symbols; entrepreneur; and visionary who believes in miracles but stands firmly on the ground.

Her mission is to encourage people and give them strength, hope, knowledge, and tools to become the best version of themselves.

https://attractionsymbols.com/

https://www.facebook.com/attractionsymbols/

https://www.instagram.com/attractionsymbols/

Practice Gratitude 123

by Mehrnaz Dehmiri

Thank you for stopping by to read this chapter. You are in for a real treat because what I am going to share with you has the potential to change your life, it really does. There may be things you have heard or haven't. All I ask is that you have an open mind because a closed mind can't accept new ideas. And really all of this is about you.

In his book, "The Science of Getting Rich," Wallace D. Wattles says, "The entire process of mental adjustment and atonement can be summed up in one word, gratitude." The first time I heard this, I thought, I am a grateful person, and I was saying what I was grateful for every day. Studying further, I learnt that writing ten things I am grateful for daily is extremely powerful, and I started this habit with my partner. We wrote about things we were grateful for that had already happened and things in the future. I learnt that the magic was not in writing or saying; it was when you felt it with deep emotions.

The second step in the process of gratitude is appreciation. Ask yourself, how would I feel if I did not have this thing, and then connect with that feeling. Once I started being thankful and appreciating all that I had and will be having, things started to shift in my life; and I attracted uplifting, abundant, prosperous, and awesome individuals. It's like the Universe opened the gate of love.

I continued to study this law and soon learnt that the highest level of gratitude is generosity. I started asking empowering questions such as, am I generous with myself? Do I spend or give my time and money freely from my heart? I realized there was much to improve. A perfect example of a generous person is Randi Goodman, whom I am extremely grateful to from my heart. Remember that writing causes thinking, thinking causes images, and images stir emotions, which in turn, cause action which equals better results. Know the best is yet to come!

 Mehrnaz Dehmiri is the founder of Good Thoughts Consulting. She believes all of us are born with infinite potential. What we choose to think and do each day determines our results. It starts with a decision but requires a success system and a mentor to create and maintain lasting change.

https://www.facebook.com/Good-Thoughts-Consulting-138274363496694

http://goodthoughts.thinkingintoresults.com

https://www.linkedin.com/in/mehrnaz-dehmiri-899ba187/

Gratitude Groove

by Meyosha Smiley

The joy ride of recognizing something to be grateful for each and every day has had an overwhelming impact upon my life. One begins with changing one's mindset in daily life from a negative outlook on things into a fondness for positive examples of existence. From the sound of a whistling bird to the thumping of an excited heart, I can always find something to be grateful for. Throughout my life, I've always tried to identify the good in every situation and with over 2000 daily gratitudes written in the past five years, I'm excited to share the inspirational factors that motivate me on a daily basis. I welcome you to join me on this journey and hope you can embrace those special moments you experience in life too.

Who am I? Imagine a beautiful, newborn baby bastard who was spared from being bounced around the foster care system because she was blessed with two wonderful parents eager to adopt her! This lucky little Chicago girl was raised in Hyde Park, the melting pot of diversity. My family taught me right from wrong, to love my neighbor, and to be grateful for my daily blessings.

What keeps me going? Do I dare admit that growing pains were confusing, and I didn't always want to be thankful? Good, strict discipline and faith were instilled to the point where I would automatically discipline myself—perhaps that's why I'm borderline obsessive-compulsive! Maturing from a child to an adult, morals and values always exceeded naughty temptations. Volunteering and offering assistance were automatic, and although I lost myself in the mix for a while, I remained grateful for every experience and lesson learned.

Where and when did it happen? Early childhood education wasn't enough. My University of Chicago social service MA was challenging, but something was missing. The persistence to earn the credentials, the drive to teach was there, but the desire to teach others on a broader level to appreciate life every day despite the circumstances? Bingo! How? I needed a hobby and daily gratitudes were born.

Why? It's a way of life!

 Meyosha Smiley (Mimi) is a native Hyde Parker from Chicago, Illinois. She obtained a BA from Chicago State University in early childhood education, and an MA from the University of Chicago, in social service administration. Mimi lives by the motto, "Be a reflection of what you receive."

https://gratitudegroove.com/

The Time is Now:
May the Real Me Come Forward

by Nadine Spencer

It was a time of darkness where nothing made sense.
Darkness that fit like a glove painted on.
Days turned into weeks, weeks into months, and months into years with
no light in sight.

Day in, day out, I wondered, how will I get out of this box I put myself in?
I know that I need help, but what does that look like again?
Who? What? Where? When do I take the steps to move forward and
get out?

I asked myself, who do I blame and what shall their sentence be?
Who is responsible to clean up this mess anyways?
Oh, it's mine, it's me, I heard my own voice say.

I put one foot in front of the other and slowly walked outside.
I walked outside of the box that held the truths of my darkness.
Pain, hurt, betrayal, rejection, lies, secrets, tears, brokenness,
abandonment.

I made the decision to get free. I knew that it would start with God leading me!
Evil fought hard for me to stay attached to the box of darkness. It whispered several times that it owned me. I told it to go back to hell!

The sun is so bright and the warmth of its rays bless me.
I have broken free from the bondage that held me.
I choose freedom to laugh, sing, play, love, leap, hug,

Pray, read the good book, rebuild, have faith, inspire others to greatness, Think positively, speak truth, walk in the truth, annihilate the lies, and say good-bye to the past me! Time is her friend.

The mirror's reflection is a dream come true. She is beautiful, radiant, alive, thriving, loving, living out her greatness, pouring truth into others to replace their darkness. Business woman, ministry leader, mother of seven, author, and relationship marketer.

The world is on it's feet cheering and applauding as she graces the platform of a new day of her new realigned life!

Here she is. She is me!

Nadine Spencer is known for being able to express truth that makes you think deeply, get understanding and be empowered. She coaches with the perspective that is always mindset changing. She helps to bring clarity using solutions to help with the discovery process through her One II One Connexion Coaching.

Contact: oneiioneconnexion@gmail.com

My Precious Child

by Nancy Yacoub

I heard about this fellow who lived a long time ago
He wasn't so normal, He had this sort of glow
He had compassion for the sick, the blind, and the lame
And He would sit amongst them and they would hear Him speak

And He'd say:
Talk to Me…Speak to Me…I know when you're hurting
Give Me your worries, your troubles, your trials
I will protect you and never forsake you
Just come to Me my precious child

I was told that He still loves amongst us today
Healing and giving life, I was filled with dismay
How could a man like Him with power be so kind
Then I heard His voice, His whispering in my heart

And He said:
Talk to Me…Speak to me…I know that you're hurting
Give Me your worries, your troubles, your trials
I will protect you and never forsake you
Just come to Me my precious child

So, I got out of bed having much to do that day
But I knelt on my knees and started to pray
With tears I felt like spilling out my heart
He put His arms around me and gave me a great big hug

And So, I:
Talked with Him…Spoke with Him…He knew I was hurting
I felt the peace, the pureness in His heart
He promised to protect me and never forsake me
I felt so safe and secure in His arms

Jesus Christ, God's only Son
Came to earth and died for everyone
He sacrificed His life so that you and I could live
And to those who believe in Him … life He'll give
Now He's in heaven … exalted high
Seated upon the right hand of God
Watching and waiting for you Dear Friend
To take His hand and simply do as He says

And He says:
Talk to Me…Speak to Me…I know that you're hurting
Give me your worries, your troubles, your trials
I will protect you and never forsake you
Just come to me My precious child

Just come to Me…Keep your focus on Me…I'll give you peace…My
precious child

Nancy is a credit professional. When she was seven, her parents suddenly divorced. She clung to the promises written in the Bible and used a pen and paper as her way to pour out her heart to her heavenly Father. Today, her poems and songs are used in various venues.

LinkedIn: http://linkedin.com/in/nancy-yacoub-bba-ccp-18998631

Contact: Nancoub@hotmail.com

Make Your Move

by Naomi R. Hall

Empowerment. I never knew the word. I never understood the word. Hell, I never took the time to. For years, I allowed another human being to define my value. He told me, "You will never be good enough. You will never be skinny enough. You don't offer anything in this relationship." Sounds crazy now, since I have someone in my life who wouldn't dare say those things to me. I'm surrounded by appreciation. I'm surrounded by beautiful. I'm surrounded by a family who truly does value me. And for the first time in my life, I feel empowered.

I spent over five years in a very emotionally abusive relationship. It was dreadful from year one. Why did I stay? Some people don't understand and never will. That's okay because the day I understood empowerment was the day I left. I left because I finally realized that I was valued.

My son was ten months old. He valued me as his mother. He valued me as his mentor. He valued me as his best friend. He valued me as a strong woman in his life. And he didn't even know it yet. I finally realized the only way I could raise a healthy, happy boy was if I was happy. He guided me to make the scariest, happiest, most empowering move in my entire life.

I packed up my things, his things, and we left. I never looked back. Not once! I will never let someone else define my value. I will never let someone tell me that my purpose on this earth is anything but huge. I am here to make moves. I am here to give value and empower other women to know that they are worth this life. They are worth this journey.

Make your move.

Naomi Hall is a mom, wife, and online entrepreneur from Orange County, California. The things she loves most are her four beautiful children, her husband, and empowering women to find their inner badass. When she's not working with clients, she enjoys fine dinners with her husband, and a good martini.

https://www.instagram.com/theladyboss.collective/

https://www.facebook.com/TheLadyBossCollective/

https://www.theladybosscollective.com/

From Shelter to Suicide Thoughts to SUCCESS

by Nathylee Harrison

After the death of my aunt, life seemed to fall apart. The type of bond I had with this aunt was one that is shared between a mother and daughter. I was also separated from my husband. A few days later, I was in jail for an assault charge. In January 2016, I called my sister. "Josie, I can't take this anymore. Nothing is going right; I don't even know who I am or where to start. Call this number and someone will find me in the bathroom." This was it. No point living. She calmly said, "I'm glad that you called me. This only proves how together you are even though it doesn't seem like it. You're my sister. I love you. Go outside, get fresh air, and Cherene will be there to pick you up. Love you, bye."

"Now answer with the first thing that comes to your mind," Cherene said. We were back at her office doing neuro-linguistic programming (NLP) therapy. That day changed my life thanks to my two sisters. Since then my husband and I are back together. You can't expect different results when repeating the same things. I wasn't doing the same things but the reasons why I thought I needed it to be done a certain way needed to change. I needed to push aside being independent and strong, and having control. Leap! That's what I needed to do.

My mom always said to me, "Trust in God. Prayer changes everything." I used to think she only said that because she's a pastor and that's what they all say but she was right. An exercise I learned was to ask myself, is the energy I'm outpouring on any situation worth it? How will it affect me in the future? Will this matter a year from now? And, will it stop me or get me closer to my end result of success? After asking myself those questions I found I was only going to be taking on negative energy that I did not need or want. That's when I found my SUCCESS!

Nathylee Harrison is wife to Nicardo Harrison, and the mother of six beautiful children: Dre'Anna, E'Lisha, Nicoi, Zion and Cairo. She owns NicNats Events & Catering, the one-stop-shop for all events and wedding needs. Nathylee is a strong individual who does not stop at anything to reach her goals.

https://www.nicnatseventscatering.com/

From Surviving to Thriving

by Neelam Dhall

I was raised by wonderful parents who guided me to do what I was supposed to do: graduate from university, build a career, get married, and have a family. So, I did, and the universe was supposed to reward me with a smooth life—or so I thought.

The universe had other plans.

We got married and were blessed with our first child. I miscarried our next child. This tragedy was heartbreaking, but we were blessed with another child and life was good again. All was going smoothly until my son fell ill. He endured five surgeries by age six. It was terrifying.

After my son recovered, my marriage fell apart. But in my culture, we don't get divorced; I couldn't stress my parents or children with a divorce. Unfortunately, circumstances showed me I had no choice.

The stress of the divorce was brutal; I felt lost and helpless. Then, ten months after separating, I was diagnosed with cancer. I was only thirty-seven. I cried thinking about my babies, but Mom reassured me that everything would be okay. I had young children who needed their mother, so I had to beat this for them. I had to save my parents from the anguish of losing a child. I had to stay strong.

So began the battle of my life. There were days I questioned my mortality, but my children's beautiful faces kept me going. Cancer puts life in perspective; it makes you see what is important and what your purpose is.

Post-treatment, I came across information on becoming a mediator. I realized that this was my life's purpose and passion; to use my life experiences and education to help others. Interestingly, within weeks, I was restructured out of my job. So, I went back to school to become an accredited family mediator. I'm now blessed and fulfilled in my work of helping others.

Life is far from smooth, but I have learned to go with the flow, listen to my intuition, and seek out the silver lining. Above all, I have learned that I can thrive no matter what happens..

Neelam Dhall is a CPA, CA, and an accredited family mediator. She is the president and CEO of Simple Solutions Mediation Ltd. Her background in finance and family law enables her to assist clients with obtaining a resolution to their divorce matters in a fast, affordable, and amicable manner.

https://simplesolutionsmediation.ca/

https://www.facebook.com/SimpleSolutionsMediation/

https://twitter.com/SimpleSolnMedn

https://www.linkedin.com/in/neelamdhall/

https://www.instagram.com/simplesolutionsmediation/

https://www.youtube.com/channel/UCjPO6JUwzKeiqns_Dg6QufQ

Life and Death

by Nicole Devcic

I was twenty years old and dating the love of my life. Everything was perfect. Until a drunk driver in a stolen vehicle hit him head-on and took his life.

The night before his accident there was a nasty snow storm. I begged him not to leave. I told him something didn't feel right. I had this unexplainable fear; it was the worst feeling of my life. I felt like something bad was going to happen. But thank god, he made it home. It was the next day, when the roads were clear, that he died.

What followed was more sorrow than anyone should experience, but death wasn't done with me yet. In 2009 my husband took his own life. Our three kids were with me the day he hung himself. That was the morning I heard a voice in my head. It was him, saying, "I have nothing to live for."

His family blamed me, and I found myself with the stigma of two tragedies. I worried about my kids. About the gossip. I was going down an unstable mental road. I knew I had to make a choice to be strong for my kids. So, I made the choice to live, to put myself and the kids first. I read books like Eat, Pray, Love and The Secret. I meditated. I spent hours walking. I ate healthy, cutting out sugar, meat, and dairy. I learned about essential oils. Eventually the fog lifted.

Now I see clearly and listen to the instincts I once brushed aside; the feeling that something bad was going to happen. My husband's desperate voice. It's taken me over forty years, but I've finally learned to listen to my intuition.

Nicole Devcic is a mother of three, loss survivor, home-based business owner, and mental health advocate. She is on a mission to keep sharing and to keep people talking, especially our youth.

www.nicoledevcic.com

Chasing Dreams

by Nicole Fyfe

I've never been one to do things for myself since having children. Everything was always centered on them and what they needed, pushing me to the backburner. So, deciding to go back to school was hard for me. It was the cause of many fights and arguments in our house, but I decided to do it anyway. I'm not going to lie, it was one of the hardest things I've ever had to do.

Going to school for eight hours a day, having homework when I got home, running a household with two active children, and having no help with all the daily things that had to be done was not easy. Plus, there were all the things that I had no control over, like when the baby was sick and throwing up and I was up all night with him, but I had an assignment that had to be handed in the next day. Then I had to put him in the car so I could go and hand in my assignment and not lose marks on it. That was a reality that happened more than once. There were nights when I had little to no sleep and days that seemed like they were never going to end. But I ended up graduating with honors.

When I walked up on that stage and accepted my diploma and saw my kids cheering and clapping for me, looking so proud of me, it made all the struggles worth it. It was then that I realized that doing for myself something that will improve me, and my children's lives is not taking me away from them. It is me showing them that if you want to be a successful and productive person in this world you have to fight and make sacrifices for a little bit, but you get to reap the benefits for a lifetime.

Nicole Fyfe is a single mother of three beautiful children ages eleven, seven, and two. She is working on obtaining her license as a pharmacy technician. Nicole is also an unpublished author who enjoys reading and watching sports when she has free time.

Charming Eternity

by Nicole Goudreau

Do you remember as a child, chatting with your friends and saying that when you got older, you were going to get married and have kids? Me too! That's exactly what I did, but what I didn't envision was receiving a diagnosis from Toronto's Sick Kids Hospital for my little girl. I became depressed until I found a charity where connecting with others and dealing with the same trials and tribulations became part of my healing process. Before the diagnosis, I was a robotic mom, waking every day doing the same thing, being the best mom I could be. I was always quiet and shy, but I became a strong advocate for my daughter, and she has taught me so much about myself that I didn't know I had in me.

I'm in awe of my daughter; she struggles every day to do what comes naturally to most people. She is one tough kiddo at times. I truly believe that she will be an incredibly strong woman one day and her strength will bring her great things. Until then, she helps me grow older and wiser, but when she wraps her arms around me and tells me she loves me, it is the greatest feeling ever.

I cannot count all the medical practitioners she's seen in her short life. We are going the natural healing route now and loving the journey thus far. I've recently become a Reiki master teacher and purged all the chemicals in our home, replacing them with all-natural, plant-based products from Melaleuca Inc. It gives me peace of mind when my girls help to clean our home and use all-natural essential oils to assist in our healing.

My amazing teenager tucks me in at night and senses when I'm having a tough day. I am blessed to have such a kind, caring, wonderful daughter, who asks me for hugs and tells me she loves me. My life has been full of challenges, but I've learned to shield myself from the negativity and remain positive with what life throws at me, counting my blessings.

Nicole Goudreau is a Christian who owns Charming Eternity. She operates as a holistic practitioner with Reiki master teacher certifications, offering cupping therapy including gua sha expertise; and mastery of essential oil blends. Nicole studied culinary management and business marketing in college and volunteers with various charities dear to her.

https://charmingeternity.ca/

https://www.facebook.com/charmingeternity/

https://www.instagram.com/charmingeternity/

Gratitude

by Nicole Scott

Five years ago, I met a family that changed my life. That family was a thief in the night and it came to steal, kill and destroy.

It's the tenant-from-hell story where the tenants refuse to pay and move out. I'm part of the family that fell victim to their entitlement and the government's inefficiency. The rules and regulations from filing notices and mediation, to securing a trial date and deferrals, would bankrupt any person in distress.

The first year we would receive notices within a day of the rent being due explaining why it wouldn't be paid. By the second year, no notice and no rent was the norm. Day by day, we watched our savings disappear while our credit cards and line of credit increased. This family brought us to rock bottom. It cost us dearly in financial devastation, marital tension, depression, a nervous breakdown, and the like.

Then something happened. It happened during one of the darkest nights of my soul, when shame and self-pity hovered near. Our money was all gone. Surrounded by complete ruin I heard a small voice whisper "thank you." Two small words triggered the deepest well in my soul causing it to erupt with gratitude. Like the blast of a mighty firework, sparks of vibrantly coloured thankfulness showered down upon me. The minute it touched me it rushed in like a flood to all the broken places and powerfully sucker-punched the adversity. The grace of gratitude was monstrous. It enveloped me with its nurturing arms. Gratitude became the antithesis to my self-pity, sorrow and depression. It instantaneously began reprogramming my brain and my heart.

Practicing gratitude has become a daily ritual. In high stress moments, it becomes the very combat weapon I use. By practicing gratitude, I successfully held the tenants accountable for their actions and received a ruling in my favor. Gratitude has become the very cornerstone of my makeup. It is the lens through which I view the world. My practice begins the minute my eyes open to the new morning that awaits me.

Nicole Scott is a visionary, wife, and mother who lives life with impact. In 1999 she co-founded SYMBIOS, now Horizon Initiative, a not-for-profit organization that empowers orphaned children to self-sustainability. In 2017 she launched a company called Modern Recreation Inc. destined to re-define coffee, people, culture, and collective recreation.

modrec.cc

Just When I Thought My Life Was Over

By Odette Laurie

Ugh, I can't get comfortable and I can't sleep!" I yelled into the empty bedroom. Exasperated, I flopped back down on the bed. Just go to sleep Odette! It was nearly midnight and I had to wake up at 5 a.m. to make the hour-long drive to take my daughters, Michaela and Briana, to school. Sleep finally came and relieved me of the life I called hell.

But my dreams didn't take me to heaven; they only replayed, night after night, month after month, the same reel of a horror movie that had become my life.

Scene one started with my blended-family-of-seven, common-law husband asking us to leave. "It just isn't working out," he said. Scenes two, three and four covered a six-month span in which Mom and Dad, both in their 80s, died within two months of each other. I was an orphan at the age of forty-four. My past and my future wiped out in one fell swoop.

As usual, I woke up that winter morning in a fog from a place I couldn't really call sleep, not knowing that life had one more surprise in store. I couldn't get out of bed because I couldn't move. Wow, I must have slept funny; my arms are asleep, I thought. I winced in frustration, but the demands of life had finally taken their toll; balled-up tension pinching the nerves in my neck, had left me paralyzed in my arms and hands.

For the next eighteen months, I endured painful rehabilitation to regain the use of my arms. I also battled extreme fatigue, feelings of failure and despair, and the fear and overwhelm of being on my own again as a single mother. Crazy as it may seem, I started a business in all of that muck and it saved my life. Despite all that happened in those few years, something amazing emerged—the real me. A stronger me. How did I do it? Support, love and belief in myself that I could overcome anything. Your turn.

After building a seven-figure business, Odette Peek suffered a personal crisis that risked it all. By sharing her story, she regained her momentum and created massive success. Odette has spoken on hundreds of stages including TEDx, popular podcasts including Entrepreneur on Fire, and television shows like NBC's Real Talk.

Website - https://OdettePeek.com

Instagram - https://www.instagram.com/odette.peek/

Facebook - https://www.facebook.com/odettepeek/

Twitter - https://twitter.com/OdettePeek

LinkedIn - https://www.linkedin.com/in/odettepeek/

YouTube Channel - https://www.youtube.com/channel/UC5ZZyED2KJFXqI059PQQGiQ

Take a Detour from the Rat Race

by Orvis McDowell

Do you feel you're always stuck on busy?

Are you always saying you have no time or money?

How would you like to see yourself finally free from that rat race?

That was me before I slowed down—juggling too many things, stressed at making a living and nothing left to make a life. It kept me from seeing how precious my life was and how wealthy beyond measure I already was. I had to get hit in the head with an airbag on highway 401 for me to see what mattered. My wife and three children were what really mattered and the source of my wealth.

After my accident, I returned home to the sound of our baby daughter crying. I never heard her cry like that before. It was different, like a piece of music from Mozart. Her cry made me smile and opened me up to find tranquility and gratitude in these priceless moments.

Being constantly busy steals your focus and blinds you from living with purpose. It's a syndrome that affects 97 percent of the population, so what secret does that other 3 percent know? It's simple, but it took a hit on the head for me to tap into it: Change your state of "busyness" and unlock your wealthy life.

Busy is a state, and changing your state is like a reset button on your life. Your priorities become yourself, your wife and kids without you dropping the ball on your other responsibilities. Otherwise it's just like when a computer gets overloaded and crashes; you take on too much and your life and family crashes too.

Having applied the secrets of that 3 percent myself, I now help Busy Dads detour their state from busyness to wealthy by changing their mindset so they can tap into the happy, healthy and wealthy life that awaits them, through my "Wealthy Dads" program.

 Orvis McDowell is a world-class, neuro-linguistic programming (NLP) coach; hypnosis trainer; speaker; author; and entrepreneur with over twenty years of business experience channeled through WealthyDads.com to inspire and transform busy dads. He is also a dedicated husband, and father of three beautiful children.

https://www.wealthydads.com

https://orvismcdowell.com

As Tears Gone By

by Paul Ciaravella

I have experienced many challenges from childhood until now, but I am living with persistence, and nothing will stop me.

When I was three years old playing outside with other children at a local farm, a horse was running loose, and all three children were run down. I was very unfortunate; my shoulder was broken, which traumatized me until the age of eight. I couldn't finish a sentence.

Later in life, I was shy, and when it was time to play soccer or baseball, I was picked last. As a teenager going on dates the same thing happened. Girls would say things like, what would you do to us, you are not man enough for us, you don't have what it takes, and I walked away from them. As years went by, I always ended up with mediocre jobs—at retail gas stations, or as couriers.

After a while I went into sales, and that was my break. My shyness went away. I met my wife, at work, got married, bought a house, and moved to Richmond Hill. We started a family and adopted a few pets. When our first child was born, the baby was ill, and we took him to Sick Kids Hospital in Toronto where they diagnosed him with an incurable disease. He lived to be one. The following year we tried again, and the same thing happened. He lived eight months.

Money was getting tight, so I started my own business. Wrong. I was a rookie and didn't know how to run a company. Money went fast, expenses were high, and to save the company I used my house and managed to lose it. I was forced to go bankrupt.

More years went by, and in 2008, I was diagnosed with Parkinson's. My doctor noticed I had tremors and put me on levodopa, a drug that messes you up with symptoms like gambling, the urge for sex, or the urge for suicide. I keep these under control thanks to my friends and their help. As I said, I live with persistence and nothing will stop me.

Nutrition coach Paul Ciaravella's passion is helping people. He's called a kaka coach because he helps those that are bloated and constipated—and he's pretty good at it! Paul's extensive knowledge of organic food and how the body works helps people have a better food system.

The Positive Well-being

by Paul Ciaravella

In 2008 I was diagnosed with Parkinson's disease and my life was crushed, my life was over. At the time it sure felt that way. I almost invited depression, but I know better than that.

One evening we had a discussion and come morning we all decided a plan of action was important to the family. In spite of the little that I knew about this, I pushed the positive self-talk and began this journey.

We scheduled an appointment with a naturopathic doctor and after the examination he assured positive results. This is a lesson that all of us must learn: surround yourself with only positive people and you will go a long way.

Sometime in the spring I met a retired doctor. She knew about nutrition and she helped me understand what I was up against. We did a major detox and talked about how certain foods can produce results. She respected me and how much I knew, and things are better for me today.

In November 2017 I dedicated this short story to the people with Parkinson's. There are alternatives to get better. For instance, when someone asks me, "How are you Paul?" my reply is, "If I was any better my health wouldn't be able to stand it."

Very well, you should know this is my way of thinking, my mindset. My downs are higher than most people's ups, and now you have read The Positive Well-being.

Cheers.

Nutrition coach Paul Ciaravella's passion is helping people. He's called a kaka coach because he helps those that are bloated and constipated—and he's pretty good at it! Paul's extensive knowledge of organic food and how the body works helps people have a better food system.

I Am Beauty

by Pauline Smiley

It was a sunny October day when I landed at Dorval airport to greet this great country called Canada for the very first time. I was still a child and highly anticipating a homecoming with hugs and cheers, but on the contrary I was met by a family friend who greeted me with these words: you are ugly. I immediately accepted his truth and it shaped my teenage years. However, as an adult this experience has spurred me to see magnificent beauty in others and to develop an appreciation for culture and diversity.

Beauty is generally defined as something that appears aesthetically pleasing to the eye. Ugliness is defined as being not aesthetically pleasing to the eye. It is therefore a matter of personal interpretation, preference and opinion as to how we define what we see. Clearly, I cannot change the arrogant world view that interprets the uniqueness in God's creation as something other than beauty. I can however define beauty as who I am.

Each of us has a uniqueness about us that defines us. Our physical attributes facially and otherwise are some of the individual traits that set us apart. Beauty is not limited to facial features because we are much more than skin, complexion, and bone structure. How about the bigness of my heart; my contagious smile that changes the mood of someone who is having a bad day; my ability to be a good wife and raise an amazing family; the unselfish self that I share with others; my unwavering entrepreneurial spirit to create businesses; and my God-given sense of value, which is translated into creating a platform and support group for women in ministry around the world.

Beauty is in understanding and appreciating cultural diversity and the awe that comes with it. Beauty is allowing the wisdom that comes from a deeply spiritual place to shape my life so I can look beyond skin and into the hearts of others around me. Beauty is to love myself and share that love with others. That is who I am, and I am beauty.

Pauline Smiley, BRE, BA, is principal broker/ owner, Livewell Mortgage Plus; co-owner and president, Livewell Pathway Healthcare Services; an elder planning counselor, and certified aging in place specialist; senior real estate specialist; and founder of RIB Connection, an international support group for pastors' wives.

http://www.livewellpathway.ca

http://www.livewellmortgage.ca

Be Yourself

by Pearl Pswarayi

"The world is your oyster" was something my mother told me all the time.

Those words became my motto and helped me seize every opportunity, which led to me learning at a faster rate than my peers. But I felt like I was doing too much too soon, and I began to compare myself to them, which caused me to make some bad decisions.

Comparison is the thief of joy.

I stopped staying true to myself, and when you are not true to yourself, life will send you people who are as false as the person you are trying to be.

In 2011 I was in an abusive relationship with a man I thought loved me, but love and obsession are two different things. I got into a relationship with a man who was cocky and insecure; and emotionally, financially, and physically abusive. In 2013 he raped me, years after I broke up with him.

That event changed me. I wore a mask almost every day, so that no one could see my pain. I wanted to disappear. I shaved off my hair, hoping that when it grew back a new me would emerge.

Sometimes life will test you and send storms to see how grounded you are.

To be your true self, you have to love your true self (faults and all), and the only way you can do that is by knowing who you are through the one that created you. As we grow, we change, but the fundamentals and foundations of who we are remain.

These foundations can stem from our culture, our families, our spirituality, or our environment, but regardless of their source, we are rooted in them.

What this experience taught me was to never again compare myself to anyone.

Be yourself; it's a lot easier than trying to be anyone else.

Pearl is a dynamic, creative, and proud woman of colour whose diverse background has made her the classic definition of a global citizen. Her global mindset advocates for people to be the best versions of themselves, which is evident her works. Her interests include fashion, film-making, equal-rights activism, and branding.

Website: http://www.pearlpswarayi.com/

Twitter: https://twitter.com/pearlynator

Facebook: https://www.facebook.com/ppswarayi

Instagram: https://www.instagram.com/pearlynator/

The Whispers of My Soul

by Preeti Chopra

Part One:

Do you ever feel lost in your own skin? It feels much like trying to escape the inevitable, but there's nowhere to hide when life is coming at you from all different directions, and failure seems to be the norm in every interaction. How do you pull yourself out of a downward spiral when nothing seems to be going your way? This is exactly how I felt one dreadful day in mid-July just after I turned eighteen.

I was a student at Eastern High School of Commerce about to begin the first day of my shorthand class. I woke up at the crack of dawn to eat and begin a fast of no food and water till dusk. I was so excited to attend this summer school class as I had been grounded by my parents and this was my chance to roam freely outside our house. I grabbed my books and off I went, skipping along the way in excitement of the new day.

I got to school and was given an outline of all the different abbreviations and symbols I had to learn to get the hang of this new rapid writing method. The hot classroom made it difficult to concentrate, but it wasn't long before we were let out and I ran to meet my friends on the football field. My girlfriend Sabira took off with her boyfriend Dilbag and I was left to chat with his friend Ajay on the field bench.

Ajay was seven years my senior and an ex-professional cricket player from India. We chatted about the weather and he told me he really liked me because he had seen me on a number of occasions hanging out at the front of East West grocers where he worked. All of a sudden in the distance we saw a store clerk come running towards us yelling. "Run. Run, run, your father and brother are coming to kill you. You better run for your lives because your brother and his gang are carrying guns and knives and they are gonna kill you," he screamed.

Preeti Chopra is a mother to five wonderful children; and a speaker; author; entrepreneur; online marketer; and life coach. She uses her story to awaken people to the desires of their souls, and reignite their passions, so they take consistent actions and live into a future of their own design.

Website: https://www.passionateimpacts.com/

Contact: Preeti@passionateimpacts.com

The Whispers of My Soul

by Preeti Chopra

Part Two:

I was to be home by 12:30 p.m. and I had broken my curfew and knew my father would be very angry with me. Now I turned to Ajay in sheer panic with sweat pouring profusely down my face, arms and legs. Ajay grabbed my hand and told me to run. I was so scared that the lifelong threats of death were about to be realised. He held my hand tightly and forced me to run with him. I begged him to stop and told him to just let me think for a moment. We came upon a telephone booth on the Danforth at Pape and I told him I needed to call my doctor. He would know what to do.

I called Dr. Harvey Kline and when I explained my dilemma, he told me to go home and that the worst that could happen would be that I would get a beating and to just take it but go home. I hung up the phone and began to cry. My stomach was hungry because I was fasting, and I wasn't able to put a drop of water in my mouth to drink till sunset. Ajay pulled me out of the booth, clutched tightly to my hand and began taking me quickly along the sidewalk without speaking a word.

By the time we got to the rooming house some four city blocks away from where my father, my brother, and his gang were looking for me, I was completely petrified. All these men and women in their late twenties in the rooming house were refugees and they spoke a different language which I barely understood. My heart was racing twenty million miles a minute and my body and legs were shaking uncontrollably. I felt like I was in a hypnotic trance, yet I could hear the whispers of my soul telling me that I couldn't go back, that my fate was sealed. Hence my life took a drastic turn into a new world, full of strange sounds and rituals where negotiation didn't exist.

Preeti Chopra is a mother to five wonderful children; and a speaker; author; entrepreneur; online marketer; and life coach. She uses her story to awaken people to the desires of their souls, and reignite their passions, so they take consistent actions and live into a future of their own design.

Website: https://www.passionateimpacts.com/

Contact: Preeti@passionateimpacts.com

Uncomfortable on Purpose

by Raj Girn

Act One

Like you, I have *those* memories.
The ones that crisscross, intertwine, and stake claim on the soul.
The ones that lurk in the darkest corners of the mind.
The ones that violently breed in the deepest valleys of the heart.
Like cockroaches, they scurry in when the sun goes down.

As a child, I would fear them.
The more I did, the bigger the congregation, and the greater the impact.
They say that beyond thirty-one days continuum, it becomes a habit.
It did.
Fear became my secret best friend.
Unknown then, it came to make me uncomfortable on purpose.

Would I have declared war on the status quo without it?
Or unbound the self-deprecation that came with it?
Because of it, I rose.
From the ashes of my own Phoenix rising, I became my own 'Personal Jesus.'
How?
I asked God . . .
"Is the only way to salvation through pain?"

217

I asked myself . . .
"If God didn't give a hall pass to Krishna-Buddha-Jesus-Mohammed-Nanak, who am I to ask? Who am I to *dare* to ask?"
But I did, and He answered, and I stopped learning.
I got why they didn't ask Him. The answer had to be sought from within.

Act Two

I heard somewhere that "energy has no allegiance."
Like a genie in a lamp, you can ask for anything.
I rubbed hard and I asked loudly . . .
Only enough pain to gain wisdom.
Only enough fear to remain humble.
Only enough success to serve my calling.

With these, I built two brands . . .
ANOKHI MEDIA, to serve a uniquely marginalized community.
OPEN CHEST, to explore intelligent, provocative, relevant insights into the human spirit.

Today, I guide those who seek to manifest, hone, and own their authority.
I help build confidence as I have built mine.
Confidence coaching is my journey. Collective consciousness is my destination.

I'm uncomfortable. On purpose.

Raj Girn, multi-award-winning media, marketing, and branding expert who works with brands like L'Oréal Paris and Estee Lauder. She's The Open Chest Confidence Coach, with a show on Dash Radio and YouYube. Raj won the ICCC Female Entrepreneur of the Year Award and was featured in two books and a documentary.

https://www.RajGirn.com

https://www.facebook.com/RajGirn/

https://www.instagram.com/rajgirn/

https://www.linkedin.com/in/rajgirn/

https://twitter.com/rajgirn_

https://www.youtube.com/RajGirn

From Survival Mode to Revival Mode

by Renée Laliberté

"I'm in survival mode." We all say it. It means going through the motions, getting through the day just to get through it. But is that truly living? No! Can you change it? It may not feel like you can, but what happens if you don't?

"Survival mode" kicked in when my kids were born. In 2006, I had a newborn, a thirteen-month-old, and a four-and-a-half-year-old. In 2008, we moved and I started a new, full-time job. For several years, I had moments of being present, while mostly just hanging on. I did my best, but my ability to cope got worse and worse.

"The crash" comes without warning. The craziest part of the whole event is that even when you are in it you don't see it! Others try to help, but you think you are fine, you think you can keep going—until you can't. I had to be told to stop by my family physician. It was November 26, 2012, the day I put on my oxygen mask first.

"Recovery mode" is when you feel the pain. If you don't feel it during survival mode or during the crash, you feel it once you stop. Your body and mind stop functioning. You have a choice to make;

are you going to continue down this path or are you going to make changes? You realize you aren't doing anyone any favours by living this way. This was my wake-up call. I got help. I learned quickly that I could not move forward until my body and mind healed. It was a time for reflection, self-exploration, and evaluating circumstances, friends, career, and family. I asked, "Who do I want to be?"

"Revival mode" is a transformation stage. It involves letting go of your old self to make room for a new life. I am grateful for what happened because it helped me find my authentic self. I realigned my purpose and regained my intuition. I am fully present, appreciating life, and envisioning a future brighter than anything my old self could have imagined.

Renée Laliberte is a business owner, speech-language pathologist, and wife to her university sweetheart. She has three teenage daughters who are just as beautiful on the inside as they are on the outside. Her passions are working with kids, travel, and crochet.

https://www.facebook.com/SpeechyBird/
https://www.facebook.com/LoopsAroundTheWorld/
http://www.speechybird.ca/

Connection is Key

by Rose Turchio

Life was unbearable! I was angry, bitter, and judgmental. I consistently allowed my anger and frustrations of the previous day, week, month, year or years to completely overwhelm me in the present moment. At times I wasn't able to function. I was riddled with resentment and fear. I chose to blame others for my mistakes, my choices, my actions, and my life because I believed it was their fault. I lost all confidence, and worry was my best friend. Life was difficult, even unbearable at times.

It was as if I was waiting for a magical day when somehow, some way life would correct itself. That special day when everything would become clear and I would be free of heavy and negative feelings. The day I could finally say, I'm happy! Well, it never came. That day turned into years of frustration, disappointment, depression, anger, more resentment, low self-esteem, and debilitating fear. Not only did it not go away, but it also grew in intensity.

I realized that I was keeping my emotions locked up inside me; I never shared my feelings with anyone. I only expressed them in times of complete frustration with yelling and complaining. Unfortunately, this only made me sink deeper into despair, and the anger I never expressed became a part of me.

That was until the day I reached out for help and discovered how powerful personal connection could be. Sharing my deepest and most sacred secrets; and my pain, sorrow, and frustrations was the day I saved my life. Unconditional love and support created the space I needed to express myself and release. Opening up, sharing and releasing my "stuff" changed my life. I am now whole, and free of the invisible chains of anger, frustration and fear that once ruled my entire life.

Find your community, your tribe and your kinships. Share your emotions and never keep them to yourself. They don't belong inside you. Set them free and take that new breath knowing you are loved and not alone.

Rose Turchio is a holistic nutritionist. Rose believes that whole health includes the mind, body, and spirit. Be mindful of not only what you eat, but also what you think and speak.

Taking the Leap of Faith

by Rosemary Ghiz

Have you ever found yourself literally frozen when you have had to come to a decision to make a big move or a change in your life? I have been in that situation many times, needing to make a big change or leap into something new. For me, it was that big fear factor and then the nerves took over. Am I good enough takes over. I would procrastinate and find millions of reasons for not doing the thing. The excuses come easy and you don't do anything about it. I would easily fall back into that comfort zone.

What I have learned is that it is all about the voice in your head, your passions, and what you want. What I have learned is that whatever it is that you want, you really need to listen to that voice, and, more importantly, not listen to those naysayers. They are out there and always ready to knock you down and convince you that you are not good enough, but I have also learned that I should not listen to them.

To be honest, it has to be one of the hardest things I have had to do. I have had to tell myself that it was their story and not mine. These people did not want to see me succeed and I needed to learn to turn them off. To be truthful, in the back of your head you're thinking, what if they are right and I really can't do this thing? What if I'm really not good enough or smart enough?

What I have learned is that when I surround myself with like-minded people, successful people, and people who have achieved what it is they wanted to do, then I find myself motivated and challenged to succeed. These people even though they have already achieved success, are more than happy to help you get where you want to be. So, if you have that big decision to make, talk to people who are already doing it as opposed to people who aren't doing it.

 Rosemary Ghiz is a mortgage and real estate professional of twenty-five years and a holistic health and wealth coach. She helps clients achieve personal and financial wealth through a better relationship with their health and money; gain more control using a financial growth mindset; and become CEO of wealth freedom!

www.rosemaryghiz.com

Money and Our Relationship with It

by Rosemary Ghiz

Money is one of those things that we grow up with and believe we understand, but no one really talks about. We acquire very definite impressions around money, and we learn spending and savings habits that come from our parents' beliefs and habits. As we get older, we take these beliefs with us as we move into the world of jobs, families, incomes, and expenses. Money is a subject we are not taught outside the home but carry with us.

Unfortunately, it can be somewhat difficult to manage and understand in a world of different opinions and attitudes around how money works. Whether we grow up in very wealthy homes or ones of low income, we are all dealing with the same issues, so managing money can become daunting. But, as with previous generations, what we are taught as children is what we hold onto, and it's primarily based on scarcity.

Today, many look to professional financial advisors to help with understanding money, how to save it, invest it, and keep it for their future. I gave my savings to an advisor to invest for me, but I've learned that we really don't know much about what is happening with our money and how to protect it. I asked my advisor about the fluctuation in value of an investment and he replied not to worry about it going down, as I needed to look at it over the long term. I received my investment statements periodically but to be honest, I think many others are in the same situation and do not know about their own investments.

I have since learned that we need not necessarily become experts in financial planning, but we do need to understand and take a bigger interest in how our money is doing. While taking more of an interest I began to learn and understand more about how the banking system works and how the wealthy are able to keep more of their money. It is our own earned money and we need to take back control for ourselves.

Rosemary Ghiz is a mortgage and real estate professional of twenty-five years and a holistic health and wealth coach. She helps clients achieve personal and financial wealth through a better relationship with their health and money; gain more control using a financial growth mindset; and become CEO of wealth freedom!

www.rosemaryghiz.com

You Can't Afford the Luxury of Negative Thoughts

by Rosemary Ghiz

Have you ever wondered what your life would look like if you listened to all the negative voices around you? We all have them. The trick is not to let them take your power and dreams away.

For many of us, those voices are repeated over and over in our heads, and too often the negative ones take over the true feelings in our hearts. For example, we often seek others' advice only to be told that it won't work, or you just can't do that.

Growing up, I was told that I was not good enough or smart enough. And well, you actually start believing it and even living with that limiting belief. I was told as a teenager that I wasn't post-secondary material and that I shouldn't waste my time pursuing a career and higher education. I knew I wanted more for my life and found it hard having my dreams dismissed and crushed in front of me.

Had I listened to those voices, I wonder what my life would have looked like today. I knew in my heart that while I was not that smart in school, I needed to explore my dreams of a career. Thanks to the help of a wonderful mentor I took the leap of faith. Many years later,

I not only received multiple degrees, but also continued on to purse my career and find my strength and passions.

My career has enabled me to help individuals and families pursue their financial happiness by becoming literate about savings, budgeting, and reaching that major purchase of homeownership; and by understanding and being in control of their finances. Over the years I have become the go-to person on financial advice, and people have been able to see that achieving financial happiness is within their means.

Limiting beliefs are all around us and it's important to realize that and to take control. Understand that other people's opinions are theirs and theirs alone. Go with what's in your heart and take the leaps in life. They are sure to pay off.

Rosemary Ghiz is a mortgage and real estate professional of twenty-five years and a holistic health and wealth coach. She helps clients achieve personal and financial wealth through a better relationship with their health and money; gain more control using a financial growth mindset; and become CEO of wealth freedom!

www.rosemaryghiz.com

The Girlfriend's Guide to Divorced Girlfriends: #TGGTDG

by Sally Donovan

It was time; I had to fess up to my girlfriends that my marriage was over.

They were eager to offer support. In trying to ease their concern I jokingly suggested they drop off a casserole to the house; I mean, I was in mourning after all...for a relationship. We declared soup more appropriate here and had a few laughs over the thought. Yes, cream-filled desserts, known for their phenomenal emotional-healing properties, also made the cut.

My friends felt helpless, so why not help them help you I thought (Everything I ever learned, I learned from Jerry Maguire). Give them a list. An appreciated, read-between-the-sarcasm list of things girlfriends can do to help you through—whisper it now—*divorce*.

#TGGTDG:

Assume designated driver role for six months.
1. Buy her drinks during above DD period.
2. Never, I repeat never, look hotter than her in public.

3. Do not complain about your husband wanting to "do it" again (see number six).

4. Lose the pity face; she will bounce back. Any friend of yours will get through life lemons.

5. Withhold your right to complain about your trivial, but relevant to you issues until appropriate.

6. Listen without judgement for a three-to-six-month period.

7. Slap her in the face appropriately, after the no-judgement, three-to-six-month period.

8. Realize that sometimes when she says, "I'm fine" she is not. You need to get over there stat!

9. Be patient and understanding; your friend is still in there finding her way back.

10. Do not forget the marriage-mourning, egg drop soup.

There you have it, a list for those wanting to help you through a trying time. It is guaranteed to provide you with the assistance you will need—a much-needed smile, and a start to an honest conversation between friends.

As for me, after that conversation with my girlfriends, you know darn well there was a jar of homemade soup on my porch the following day!

Founder and author, Sally Donovan, is on a mission to support women through life transitions. A single mom with a previous career in analytics, this numbers gal turned writer has published her first in a series of guided journals, sharing perspective + humour (her favourite equation) along the way.

Happiness Comes from Within

by Samantha F. Glass

All my life I had been off, a little scared, a little shy, a little too hesitant to show my real self to the world. Always guarded, always holding back a large piece of myself for the fear of judgment from others. In my childhood, although I was very free to do a lot of the things I wanted, I was not popular, not rich. I dressed in clothing from Bi-Way while the kids in my class always had the latest clothing.

I was bullied, put down, called stupid and fat. Those words lived with me into my adulthood. I was always doubting myself, always feeling like I was never good enough, always allowing that to define me, consume me. It became me. It silently tortured me! I felt so down about myself, it came out in my relationships with everyone around me.

How could I allow words to have so much power over me, over my mind, body, and soul? I needed to change this. I started watching the world around me and seeing how negative a place it could be. I couldn't allow this to continue. I vowed to myself that I would stand up and fight to make change in myself, and in turn, change in the world.

I became a litigation paralegal and opened my own paralegal firm called SFG Paralegal Services. I now help others solve their everyday problems, and bring positive change to people's lives in some of the most vulnerable high-stress legal situations. They don't have to let things consume them and control them; they know they have someone in their corner.

Remember, happiness comes from within and spreads. It illuminates from a smile, from all that positive energy you have inside. People sense it. It is not about what you look like that defines you; it's what makes you original, interesting, and beautiful. Taking a chance and stepping outside of your comfort zone often builds confidence. You're empowered to change you! You're empowered to make a difference! You're empowered to take the negative from your life and turn it into positivity!

Samantha F. Glass is the founder of SFG Paralegal Services. Her passion is access to justice! She continues to find ways within her paralegal scope to ensure the public has representation. A very friendly and caring person, Samantha is highly skilled and fights vigorously and passionately for her clients.

Website: www.sfg.legal

The year of me!

by Sandra Didomenico

I was suffering in silence and I really did not know what the emptiness was, but it was painful. I had been a stay-at-home mom for seventeen years and I was devoted to raising my beautiful children, but in that time, I had completely lost who I was as a woman in society. I am a wife and mother first and I have domestic duties with that title, however my place in society to fulfill me was lacking. I felt unheard, no voice, emptiness, a void. I saw other women achieving, empowering, and conquering, but I felt only lack.

That is until something powerful landed on my lap—direct sales and a business model that would leverage my time and fulfill me as a woman with something of my own. I got my sexy back, my mojo and my confidence! I was a new-woman-in-training when I came across a lifestyle coach who changed everything! These two elements—direct sales and personal life coaching—may be something you're skeptical about. However, with the power of many people duplicating a business model and leaders cheering me on, I found a new love: to help and serve all those lost, unconfident women. I also vowed to work on myself. I decided that was going to be the year of me! After seventeen years of dedication and devotion to my family who did not need me as much I realized, it was my time to shine again.

Today, I am the CEO of me, powerful and confident. My passion is to be what Wallace Wattles called, "a person of increase" every single day to enlighten someone else in society. In fact, I inspire hundreds of women to feel confident again through my business as a mentor. I have taken on the simplest tools for everyday life that align me in a mindset of happy energy all day long. The power of your mind matched with the perfect practices can be applied anytime in your life. I realized I had a choice every second of the day and I chose to fuel up and drive!

Entrepreneur Sandra Didomenico is an independent market partner with Monat Global. For the past three years, she has grown a thriving business, helping thousands of women and men bring their hair back to life!

Website: https://sandradido.mymonat.com/

Instagram: https://www.instagram.com/hair_journeywithsandra/

From Fear to Freedom: My Defining Moment

by Sandra Dindayal

It was not when I lived in fear watching my dad abuse my mother; not when I married at age thirteen and gave birth to my first child at age fourteen; not even when my ex-husband came home drunk and pinned me to the floor with a machete on my neck ready to take my head off my body.

No, my defining moment was October 1, 2015, when I woke up with a sharp pain in my left jaw. Thinking it was a toothache, I failed to recognize the warning sign. I ignored the pain and went on with my daily duties taking care of everyone but myself. On day three I decided to go to the dentist to remove the tooth that I thought was hurting. It was the dentist who recognized it was a heart attack, called the ambulance and sent me to the hospital. After I woke up from my surgery I discovered I was ninety-five percent blocked in my main artery, and I realized I had been a walking dead person for three days.

In that moment, I knew that God had a plan for me, which is why he gave me a second chance in life. He wanted me to survive so I could tell my story about how I was living in shame, fear, hurt, and guilt. My story about how I carried this for all my life, hiding it in my heart.

No wonder I got a heart attack at age fifty-four; it was a complete block. But now there were no more places to hide and I vowed to God and myself to use this life to do something great.

Today, as a breakthrough and transformation coach, I work with women like myself to help them eliminate many of the problems that are buried deep within. I also coach them on how to let go of fears and take back their power. Permanently!

So what is your story? What feeling are you storing in your heart? Are you ignoring the warning signs?

Sandra Dindayal is a breakthrough and transformation coach, and entrepreneur. With over twenty years of experience, she works with women who want to get to the root of their problems. Her mission is to teach and empower women globally to bring out their inner voice and take back their power.

https://www.facebook.com/sandradindayal88

`My 10-Year Overnight Success

by Sara Wiles

One tear-filled day, I took charge of how I wanted my career and life to look. I was over the corporate grind and 24/7 emails. Mostly, I was over the stress and anxiety of not being present in my son's life.

So, I started a business that allowed me to live life on my terms, to be with my son full-time, and to replace my corporate income working from home part-time.

Have you ever been in a situation where the stars aligned and everything you asked the universe for came back to you in spades? When I opened my virtual assistant business serving other mompreneurs, that's exactly what happened.

Within eight days of starting the business, I signed my first client. Two weeks later, I left my corporate job. Another two weeks and I had the clients (and income) to replace my nine-to-five salary. Within months, I added contractors to my team, took on more clients, and exceeded my wildest financial goals. I created a course to help mothers launch their own virtual assistant businesses, my most fulfilling venture yet. And, I was finally the present, engaged mother that I so deeply wanted to be.

Now here's the part of "overnight success" that most people don't share. Prior to opening my business, I spent eight years producing high-end corporate events and a year working for a start-up. During those years, I cultivated the organizational and technical skills that made my online business success even possible. I started and ended three blogs, one health coaching business and an MLM. I failed a lot (and learned a lot) and it's only because of those experiences that I was able to see my version of wild success at the age of thirty-one.

Do you dream of creating a life and business on your terms someday? Keep going. Keep launching businesses, blogs and Etsy stores. Keep taking new corporate jobs, taking chances, learning new skills and failing. And, when the right thing comes around, because of your successes and failures, you will be ready to create your own amazing version of success.

 Sara Wiles owns a virtual assisting and event planning company. She spent years producing high-end corporate events before becoming an entrepreneur. After four weeks in her business, she replaced her nine-to-five income and brought on a team. Sara is also a mother, a champagne enthusiast, and sweat addict.

www.sarawiles.co

Our Power Within

by Sarah De Medeiros

I grew up in what seemed to be a normal home. My mother was a stay-at-home mom, and my father was a successful lawyer. My very loving sister was only slightly older than I was. When I was approximately six years old, things started to change. My mother became a severe alcoholic, my parents divorced, and my father gained full custody of me and my sister. I have only seen my mother on two occasions since I was eight years old. Unfortunately, she did not overcome her challenges.

I felt very empty, not having my mother in my life. The emptiness turned into sadness and anger as an early teen, and I began drinking and doing drugs at fourteen. At the age of nineteen, I was sexually assaulted and started to follow in my mother's footsteps. I became addicted to alcohol, and my life became very dark. By the time I was twenty-four, I was in such a dark place that I knew I had to make changes for me to survive. This could not be what life was about.

My first step towards addressing my addiction was to realize that I had to let go of the pain, the hurt, the heartache, and the anger that was rooted in my childhood. I started to realize that I had to forgive my mother and every other person that I felt contributed to my darkness, including myself.

I started to change how I looked at life and the people around me. I opened my eyes to see that others cared and the more I let go of the hurt, the easier life became. With each forgiveness, I found peace towards others and peace for myself.

I changed my inner dialogue and it became positive. Each day began with a gratitude list. I became kind towards myself. Through the power of believing in myself I have learned that I am worthy. I am deserving. I am light. I am love.

I can now transmit that love, light, and hope to others because I see it in myself.

Sarah De Medeiros is an intuitive energy healer, coach and speaker. She is passionate about helping others to bring healing to physical and emotional pain, along with guiding others to their own inner peace, emotional harmony, and spiritual wellness.

https://www.sarahdemedeiros.com/

Comfort Zones

by Sarah Mulaner

I've moved a lot—over eleven times by the age of eighteen. I went to four different high schools. My favourite place I've called home is California, but the place I truly consider to be home is Nova Scotia. I now live in Oakville, Ontario, and it's where I've raised my son.

Comfort zones are created in childhood and for me it felt "normal" to move often. If life felt stagnant or uncomfortable, I moved. Moving is disruptive, chaotic, and it encourages a sense of upheaval. A sense of instability is ongoing, and it creates anxiety and nervousness. But, it's human nature to cling to the familiar, so regular, dramatic change has become one of my adult habits.

I'm now in my forties with a teenage son. I recognize my patterns and see the drag that back stepping through life has caused. Two steps forward and one step back is slow going! I now look to create a strong foundation as I continue along, and I trust that I'll be moved in the right direction. I enjoy change and am slow to move forward, embracing the lessons as they come. There's no need to destroy and re-create. I have faith that the universe supports me and shows me what I need. As Louise Hay says, "All is well, and I am safe." I'm now shopping for my retirement home—I'm ready to put down roots and build my community.

From a foundation in the fitness industry to a busy massage therapy practice, Sarah Mulaner has been a lifelong advocate of physical, emotional and energetic health. Her patients appreciate her multi-faceted interests and wide knowledge base as she supports them in building optimal health.

http://www.imaginewellness.ca/

Necessity Is the Mother of Invention

by Sarah Mulaner

If necessity is the mother of invention, then perhaps motherhood is the force driving reinvention. Having cruised through my twenties with lots of passion and enjoyment of my career in the fitness industry, I hadn't put much thought towards finances. I've always worked hard and was happy that I loved teaching exercise classes to wonderful participants and enjoyed training clients one-on-one. Goal setting and coaching them on their path was amazing!

When I gave birth to my little bundle of joy, I had the rude awakening that I needed to approach my career path more seriously with a mind towards the bottom line. I worked part-time until my son was two and then took a salaried position managing a fitness centre. I hated it! I decided to build my business doing in-home personal training to keep my overhead down and within a year I'd created my website, hired contractors to help with workload, and had developed a six-figure business. I knew I couldn't continue as I was, and I was thrilled to become a successful business owner doing something I loved.

My son is now in high school and will be doing his personal training certification in the next year. He's seen my passion throughout his life and is eager to pursue fitness, personal training, and coaching to help others achieve their goals.

From a foundation in the fitness industry to a busy massage therapy practice, Sarah Mulaner has been a lifelong advocate of physical, emotional and energetic health. Her patients appreciate her multi-faceted interests and wide knowledge base as she supports them in building optimal health.

http://www.imaginewellness.ca/

Freedom

by Sarah Mulaner

"Freedom is not worth having if it does not include the freedom to make mistakes"
-- Mahatma Gandhi 1869-1948

I think we can agree; we've all made our share of mistakes. Some major, some minor, some life-altering. This is where we can clearly see, over time, our fears, our insecurities, and our challenges. In moving forward after mistakes have been made, we create perspective, wisdom, and strength to continue pursuing our dreams, our goals, and our truths.

I consider freedom to be one of my values, something I strive for and absolutely need to feel like I can create my own path in life. When I spoke to a lifelong friend recently, she brought up that I have constantly evolved over the twenty-five-plus years that we've know each other. She was going to say "changed," but realized that I haven't changed, I've grown and expanded. I've chosen careers, partners, and homes with some success, but I've needed to adjust my course a number of times in each area.

I now have a clearer sense of who I am, what I need, and what makes me happy. I need some structure and stability for a sense of security, but also lots of flexibility for personal expression and exploration. Can I be spontaneous? Sure! Have I messed up a time or two? Absolutely! Have I taken steps that were bold, irrevocable, and risky? Yes, and I have created a life I'm thrilled with by doing so. Freedom is a gift to use wisely, to learn from, and to take advantage of as often as possible.

From a foundation in the fitness industry to a busy massage therapy practice, Sarah Mulaner has been a lifelong advocate of physical, emotional and energetic health. Her patients appreciate her multi-faceted interests and wide knowledge base as she supports them in building optimal health.

http://www.imaginewellness.ca/

Create Your Own Path and Live Fearlessly

by Sarah Shu

Life seems so exciting yet linear when we graduate from university. In reality, it's never a straight line but rather a map of many dots and lines. We create our own paths.

In the spring of 2000, I came to Canada. Despite the frigid temperatures, I was extremely excited. My heart was pounding because my dream had come true. Canada was a place where I saw endless possibilities, freedom, and a new life. In the first two months, I had no furniture, only two suitcases packed with books and clothes, so I slept on the floor. In 2002, I graduated with a master's in engineering and received an offer from a global technology company. I felt proud and successful.

Four years later, at the passing of my grandfather and mentor, I started to examine my life as if it were about to vanish in the blink of an eye like his. I asked myself if I was happy and doing what I loved to do. Was I chasing the wrong targets? What did success mean to me? I felt I was proceeding too fast and too narrowly in my field so that my job had started to become the center if not all of my life. I was horrified to realize that I had worked so hard to achieve a life that was not true to myself but rather to what others expected of me. So, I decided to create my own path and explore my potential. I ventured out to the west and then returned to Toronto to obtain an MBA at the end of the financial crisis.

Just as I started to feel a firm grip on a new business career in 2014, I was diagnosed with cancer in one of my salivary glands. I was devastated, lost, and unsettled. I have never felt anything stronger than the desire to live. Thankfully, the surgery went well, and my life went back to normal. The lesson I learned from facing death was this: spend time on what matters to you, prioritize rigorously, and let the rest go.

Sarah Shu is the founder of Wrise Consulting. Wrise focuses on helping women entrepreneurs build business plans, turn their visions into successful businesses, and make the world a better place.

Website: www.wrise.ca

Miss Manifest

by Sarah Zoldy

Thirty-five years old and I'm still latched onto the voluptuous breast of life. Suckling away at all the nourishing adventures, knowledge, and lessons that it can provide for my growing body, mind, and soul. Will I ever wean myself off? Heck no. Not everything that comes our way is delicious and fulfilling; I too, have had my own fill of trials and tribulations. But, rather than fall victim to my life circumstances and indulge in self-pity, in my early twenties I benefited from a devastating, life- changing event in order to wake up and jump-start my life.

I could not picture myself becoming a bitter and resentful single, middle-aged woman pointing the middle finger and snarling at any man who should cross my path. After many hours of counselling and watching the video "The Secret," I started consciously practicing the science based on the laws of attraction. The day that I realized that I was the one responsible for manifesting my terrible relationships, divorce, and other things, was the first day of the rest of my life.

Whether positive or negative, our subconscious and conscious thoughts and energetic vibrations that we put out into the world are the determining factors that influence what we manifest. I had to push myself to forgive and send the power of love and positive thoughts to those who I was allowing to hurt me. Then the negative feelings started to dissipate, and life started to change drastically within only a few weeks.

I test this secret all the time, and deliberately manifest everything I want. We have more control over life than we are programmed to believe. Everything is possible! Attention deficit hyperactivity disorder (ADHD), perfectionism, negative people, abuse, divorce, single parenting —I let none of these stand in my way. If I feel impatient or discouraged when things don't happen quickly enough for me, I just latch right onto that breast of life again. Sometimes it takes a bit for the "letdown" in order for things to flow into place, but it always does. Cheers to the breast life you could ever imagine!

A sassy, charismatic, free-spirited, single mother, Sarah Zoldy has a huge zest for life. She thrives on being a role model for everyone embracing their true selves, loving life, and attracting what they truly desire. Always embarking on new adventures, she lets nothing stand in the way of her manifestations!

Candle in the Wind

by Shama Jawaid

When I was born my father decided to name me *Shama,* which in our native language means 'light of a candle.' He named me this because he said I brought light into my mother's and his life. They immigrated to Canada in 1969 from Pakistan, without any family or friends. During her twenty years in Canada, my mother never held a job or had money of her own and suffered from poor health and an unhappy marriage. Her English was broken, and she felt inadequate, unable to contribute in a strange country.

Just before I graduated from high school in 1989, she said, "If something happens to me, I want you to remember this: always be strong, make your own money, and be independent." Three months later at age forty-six, she died of a massive heart attack leaving our family in complete shock. My candle had blown out for the first time.

Fast forward to 2017. Adversity hit me head-on. The stresses of my professional and personal lives collided. For years I lived wearing a mask. Outwardly I was successful and independent, however, inside I was unravelling. I was failing in both my career and marriage. I was forced to take a leave from work and three months later, became separated from my husband. My candle had blown out … once again.

My mother spoke to me through a friend who happens to be a channeler. "Your mother is with you. She was a woman who felt small but wanted to be bigger in her life. She wants you to live your *authentic* life." I learned that it is alright to let go, that it's alright to cry, and that strength is born through vulnerability.

Today, with my mother watching over me, my candle burns brighter than ever as I stand in my own light and live my most authentic life yet. A candle is a source of light, energy, and warmth. When the wind of adversity hits your life, don't think of it as a negative force but as fuel to your flame.

 Shama Jawaid works for corporate Canada as a senior marketing manager in the tech industry and has over fifteen years of marketing experience. She is currently going through a major transformation, which is leading to a path where she can realize her passion for writing.

http://freshlysqueezeme.blogspot.ca/

Millennium Single Moms Soaring High

by Sharon Pike

Millennium single moms are forced into a world of Internet entrapment, the web of destruction. Single moms are faced with superhuman behavior and functions. All their parental skills are begin documented and governed by our new world order. Their skills to discipline, nourish, motivate, and love are taken over by a server, the Internet manual, and the information highway. The information age is catching up with single moms.

They have more than strangers to deal with, now they have Internet predators. The new world order captures our sons and daughters. The web of destruction replaces the inner connections that are needed from a mother or a father. This craving desire for attention and information is not healthy for humanity. This web of so many faces and misleading places is false advertising.

No more rushing home to cook and clean, this new device prepares your dinner and cleans up for free. The children of millennium single moms have lives that are developing so fast they never will get a chance to embrace this sudden advance. The children are being served by the fridge, motivated by YouTube, and highly inspired by the games they subscribe to or join.

Single moms on the run, how many jobs do you have to rub, just like the mouse? You serve all who come around, that's the life of a single mom, always on the run. Single moms chose a key, now it's time to break free. Single moms who clear your plugs, who remembers to give you a hug? You only know when you are tired, when you get a bug. There is no shame in a single mom's game, cause you're not here for fortune or fame.

Millennium single moms create a family, not a bunch of pickney. Our children are submerging themselves into the Internet, a brainwash system that was designed to control our emotions, desires, and set our hearts on fire. The children are faced with too many choices, so the right mindset is needed. Millennium single moms you are the captain of your ship and crew. Accountability, integrity and consistency create an amazing family.

Sharon Pike is an extraordinary person and single mother who overcomes failures and disappointments, using them as stepping stones to achieve success. She worked as a medical and endoscopic technician, always willing to go the extra mile, and now she's an upcoming author. Sharon loves nature, reading, writing, and travel.

How I Changed My World

by Sheila Messa

I thought I was well positioned to reach my long-term goal of building a comfortable nest egg for my retirement and leaving a legacy for my children and community.

I had an engineering degree, and I led innovation in digital communications for a company that was the darling of the TSX.

However, the dot-com bubble burst in 1999! I not only lost my six-figure income because the company where I was working went under, but also all the gains in my nest egg—my RRSP portfolio. My first recourse was to find another job and work my way back to my six-figure income and continue contributing to my RRSP to make up the lost gains. At that point most companies no longer offered any pension plan, so the onus was all on me to build that nest egg for my retirement years and what I desired to leave as a legacy for my family and community.

I continued that journey and got back on track until in 2007 the market crashed again. Voila! There went all the gains in my RRSP, and my portfolio value retuned to inception level. That was a massive wake-up call. I realized that if I didn't make a big change in how I was working towards achieving my financial goals, I would end up not being able to leave the legacy I was always dreaming of.

So, I began to explore other avenues. I started learning about real estate investment and realized that by following that path I would not only achieve my own financial goals, but also help others achieve their dreams of home ownership. That to me was a no-brainer. I started investing in real estate and in three years I achieved what I had not achieved in over two decades!

Now, I want to share my story and my knowledge with those who dream of home ownership but need help getting there, and who want to build a legacy for their family and community.

Sheila Messa is a real estate investor and coach, and an entrepreneur, with vast business management experience. She co-founded her real estate investment company in 2011 and grew it to over $2.5 million net worth in three years. Sheila is a BASc graduate from the University of British Columbia.

Facebook: https://www.facebook.com/Sheila.Messa1/

Instagram: https://www.instagram.com/sheilamessarealtor/

LinkedIn: https://www.linkedin.com/in/sheilamessa/

Website: https://sheilamessa.com/

Who Controls Your Thoughts?

by Sher Smith

It is so true that our thoughts are the master of the results in our life. Energy follows thought and precedes a change in structure and form—whether that is the structure and form of your body or your life. Change your thoughts and you can change your life. I heard this years ago and incorporated it into my life and teaching. The results are amazing.

It has been said that our thoughts create our actions, which then create our behaviours, which become our habits and determine our results. To change our results, we first have to change our thoughts. Remember, inch by inch is a cinch, and yard by yard is hard. What that means is take baby steps.

Choose to control your thoughts with conscious mindfulness, or your subconscious will pick up thoughts from the environment. Thoughts floating around are often negative. What weatherman gives the percentage of sunshine for tomorrow?

Sometimes it can be a challenge; but, whatever you focus on expands. When the bills are piling up your mind tends to keep thinking of them. We have to take charge, make a conscious effort to control our thoughts and find something, no matter how small, that is positive—and focus on that. Then, our awareness rises, and we draw to us more of the positive.

We need to write down our thoughts so we can see them. Then, repeat them out loud to hear them. That is when we discover whether we are being positive or not. We may find that meditation brings clarity. People who spend time in nature often get clarity. I go for a walk to find my creativity. We are often ill because in this fast-paced life, we forget to take time to be still, and that causes dis-ease in our systems.

Focusing on the positive builds a strong neural network to draw more of the same to us. In this way, we are practicing health building through the power of positive thinking, and that lifts us to realize our potential. You create your future.

Sher Smith, RN, BCPP, RCST, RPE, is the director of the Realizing Your Potential Center of Holistic and Energetic Studies. Starting as a pioneer in the field and having had years of training, Sher is now a gifted presenter and instructor. Sharing her knowledge is her passion.

www.realizingyourpotential.ca

Reflections

by Sherri-Anne Murphy

Who do you see when you look in the mirror? What story does your reflection tell?

Mine shows me a face filled with experience, a face that has had much joy and sorrow, one that has laughed and cried, frequently at the same time.

I'm thankful for all the things that make this face the one that looks back at me: the unsettled childhood—never quite feeling like I belonged or was worthy; the three marriages—ending for different reasons, but leaving me doubting myself and trying to figure out who I was; the devastating losses of my mom and my lifelong friend—both at the young age of 50, my nana who was my rock, and my favourite uncle—the one man who always believed in me. These are some of the things I see.

But I also see in my reflection the amazingly happy events I've had in my life: the birth of my beautiful daughter—on my birthday—and the strong relationship we have; the wonderful friendships I've made that have lasted many years; a great relationship with my brother and other family members; and so important to me, my spiritual journey. My relationship with the angels is strong and I've learned that asking them for help will always bring results. I've grown stronger through all those who have touched my life, whether they are physically in it now or not.

We can all look at our lives and wonder what if this or if only that. We can have regrets and hang on to things that do not contribute to our purpose. But if we can find something positive in everything we've experienced, no matter how small, we can move forward with strength.

So, who do I see? I see a woman who has lived through happiness and sadness and come out the other side, strong, loving and ready to take on more of this thing called life. Reflections are a beautiful thing. Now take a look at yours!

Sherri-Anne Murphy is a wedding officiant, inclusively joining couples in marriage, commitment ceremonies, and vow renewals. As a transition coach practitioner, she guides those who have lost their sense of themselves in relationships to a path of personal purpose. Her personal and professional HR experiences highly complement her chosen vocations.

www.sherriannemurphy.com

On Learning to Love Yourself Before Others

by Shirley Tran

You were witty, you were charming. Your light was luminous. Your love was magical. You were strong. The kind that would move mountains. You were an inspiring possibility.

You led me to believe in me and that made you a dream.

Each gentle kiss and soft touch exchanged felt endless and surreal. Every stroke, every stare, every moment sunk deeper. With every breath inhaled I took a piece of you.

How is it possible to be able to share the same air, same space with someone in such euphoria? It's compulsive, obsessive, manipulative.

I became lost in you.

How much I wish to say to you.

You lifted me up.
You spoke truth.
You cried tears.
You let me soar.
You opened up.

You let me in.
You pushed me further in places
I was never able to go in my heart,   mind, body and soul.
Then you held me close, whispered sweet nothings and started to fade.
You let good go.
You left it to die.
You let your demons win.
It was no longer about us and all about you.
I tried to hold on with all my might.
You consumed almost all of me
While allowing your darkness to consume all of you.
I almost fought for it.
I almost saved it.
I almost died trying.
But in the end I fought for true love.
The kind of love that was only found within me.
My light pushed through.
It found its way back to my inner child.
Who needed me more than it needed you.
It let true love lead the way.
It found peace.
It found sun.
It found the blue ocean.
You melted into the oasis.
There, you are no more.
We, are no more.
As much as I loved you.
I love me more.

Shirley Tran is a dreamer, visionary, and coffee lover; and a lifestyle-business branding specialist. She helps coaches and creatives design fresh and professional brands that stand out through photography and video branding; site design; and Instagram make-overs.

Instagram:
https://www.instagram.com/liveloveshirley/
https://www.instagram.com/theeverlystudio/

I Am a Hybrid, Perhaps You Are One Too

by Sibo

A few years ago, a guy broke up with me because I acted "too white."

"Wait, what? What does that even mean?" was my reaction.

It means that I do things labeled as western culture. But first, let me tell you a bit about me and you'll draw your own conclusion.

My favorite food is Korean BBQ beef ribs; my favorite song is "Vulindela" by Brenda Fassie, a South African singer; my favorite film is *Kabhi Khushi Kabhie Gham*, an Indian movie. I was born and raised in Rwanda, but when I got to the age of questioning everything, my family and I moved to Canada.

At school, everyone was doing their best to introduce me to Canadian culture, and at home, my parents were doing all they could so that I wouldn't lose my Rwandese culture. If you know the rope-pulling game, imagine me as the rope. On the verge of being torn apart, I decided I was neither Canadian nor Rwandese. I was both. I was culturally mixed—a hybrid!

I realized that it was okay to have two cultures: it was okay to choose values I wanted from each; it was okay to admit that I do not like the Rwandese popular dish, Isombe n'Ubugari; and it was okay not to be what my family expected me to be, or what society influenced me to become.

Many studies prove that knowing two languages gives cognitive benefits but having two cultures is even better. It's a huge privilege! My goal now is to help others who feel like they do not belong to realize their potential and guide them on how to be the person they choose to be.

I started a program that focuses on giving children and youth strategies on how to develop skills of confidence and courage. It helps them get more self-esteem and a sense of belonging among people they can relate to. This program is for immigrants, children of immigrants, their friends and anyone willing to learn about other cultures.

Sibo is a great friend. She is best friends with her siblings. She is friends with her ex-boyfriends. She is friends with her neighbor who calls her granddaughter. She is a snap friend to strangers crying in public. Why? Because she cares and understands the lack of connection people face.

Blog: http://dearsibo.com/

Website: http://hybridsafezone.com/

Young and Empowered

by Sophia Procopio

I am about to turn twenty-five with my whole life ahead of me. And yet, I feel I haven't accomplished enough for my age. Why do I feel that way? Growing up, I was depressed and insecure about my family, friends, relationships, education, career, and body. When I was eleven, my parents unfortunately divorced and my father left the country to start a new journey. This took an emotional toll on my life and more specifically, my school work. I found myself acting out in school and taking my anger out on everyone around me.

However, this difficult experience also made me more independent and mature at a young age. And what kept me distracted and passionate during this time was dance! I danced up to five times a week at the competitive level. In the first few years of my undergraduate degree I began working as a recreational and competitive dance instructor and choreographer. I fell in love with working with my students because I was able to see them progress and grow throughout each dance season. That was when I knew I wanted to become an elementary school educator. So, I did it; I am now an Ontario certified teacher!

After teacher's college I realized that I wanted to combine my two passions: education and dance, so I decided to develop my own dance company, On the Move Dance. On the Move is a mobile company that educates students from Kindergarten to Grade 8. The company teaches students a variety of dance styles including jazz, hip hop, contemporary, and musical theatre; and offers pre-developed lesson and unit plans, assessment sheets, and a teacher in-service program. On the Move Dance is currently contracted in school boards throughout the Greater Toronto Area, and is expanding throughout Canada. The most important part of my company is ensuring that students are engaged, comfortable, and safe. Dance has always been my outlet throughout problematic times in my life, and I hope my story can inspire many individuals going through similar experiences.

Sophia Procopio is an educator, business owner, dance instructor, and food blogger. She is currently working on her third degree, a master's in education; and recently developed a mobile dance education company entitled, On the Move Dance. Sophia is passionate, dedicated and motivated throughout all of the work she does.

onthemovedance.com

Faith Can Conquer Fear!

Stacey Ann Berry

For years I kept my talents locked in a box because of fear. I treated them like my best-kept secret. I was fearful of being judged, mocked, and rejected. I did not think I could rely on my talents to survive economically. My perspective changed one cold winter day in 2013, when I was laid off from what I thought was a secure job. That unfortunate circumstance became a blessing in disguise.

Being unemployed forced me to look deep inside myself, take an inventory of all my skills and talents, and create a plan. I decided to narrow my focus and develop one talent at a time. In 2015, I launched my company, Bstellar Consulting Group but struggled to make it sustainable. I remained open to new opportunities to grow my skills but needed a full-time job to have a stable income.

After receiving over 700 rejections to job applications, and knocking on unopened doors of potential clients, my faith was tested. When I surrendered to divine intervention, I was able to rely on my talents, have greater confidence in my abilities, and trust God completely. In 2016, I secured my biggest client, and by 2017, I landed a full-time job. Being an employee and an entrepreneur is not easy to balance, but it allows me to enhance my skills and gives me tremendous value.

Faith is the foundation of my success. I rely on it to transform my ideas into reality, conquer obstacles, adopt a winning attitude, and take risks. Having faith in a power higher than myself keeps me grounded and gives me reassurance that I am not alone. It also changed my view of success, which I no longer define as having material wealth or accolades. True success is having inner peace and joy in the midst of struggle and challenges. It means believing that the sun will shine after the storm. If you want to make your dreams a reality and maximize your potential, do not let fear hold you back; step out in faith, and your true purpose will manifest. Your destiny awaits you!

Stacey Ann Berry is the founder and CEO of Bstellar™ Consulting Group, which provides soft skills and community development workshops; and consulting services in government relations and event management. Stacey is a member of various non-profit organizations and has a master's in public policy administration and law from York University.

The Amazing Power of Gratitude

by Stacey Grewal

In 2006, life as I knew it turned upside down.

My husband lost his business and was forced to declare bankruptcy. The bank foreclosed on our home, our car was towed away, and the government was demanding an insane amount of back taxes. We were in debt up to our eyeballs, and at times there was barely enough money to buy groceries.

I fell into a cycle of self-pity, resentment, and blame. I was angry with my husband because he had ruined my life. I resented my children because they were holding me back from exploring my dreams. I blamed my parents because they were such poor examples. Now, not only were we broke but also our marriage was on the brink of destruction.

Then I watched the movie, *The Secret*.

Its message was one I had heard before but wasn't ready to receive until then. This is what I heard:

You are in control of your destiny. You must change your way of thinking and behaving if you want to change your life for the better. Positive thought reaps positive reward. No one can save you. You have to save yourself. Gratitude is the key!

I began to practice gratitude throughout my day, every day. With this simple shift from an attitude of self-pity to one of abundance, I instantly became the master of my destiny.

I began to rethink our family's circumstances, taking responsibility for my part in the way things had turned out. Lo and behold, my life unexpectedly began to blossom in so many beautiful ways.

Gratitude gave me the confidence to want to do more, be more, and have more in my life. I knew that if gratitude, applied the right way, could help me make such a life-altering change, it could help others do the same. I decided to take action and follow my dreams.

Since then, I've been teaching people all over the world how to use the amazing power of gratitude to live happier, more joyful, more purposeful lives.

Stacey Grewal is a life coach and spiritual mentor. She is the author of the book, Gratitude and Goals. To find out more about Stacey and receive access to her free training, check out her website.

www.staceygrewal.com

Never Give Up on Your Dreams

by Stacey King

My life has struggles and heartaches, but I have always had a vision and dream to be successful no matter what people believe and say about me. I know it's going to be a hard road, but I believe in myself and my God to help me become what I want to be. I am a powerful and strong woman and hopeful to become better in my life for me and my kids. Being a single mother of eight kids was not easy at all, but let me tell you, you can do anything you want in life no matter what. Read Proverbs, chapter one—put your trust in God, and he will lift you up in your time of need.

On May 12, 2018, I met Les Brown in person and that was one of the best moments in my life. It opened my eyes to a lot of things and gave me a lot of hope about my dream. He told me to never give up on my dream and passion, and to never quit. He also told me that if your life was easy then it's not a good thing; you must work for things.

Here's a poem that I wrote:

Never give up on your dream,
Always have faith in yourself,
Believe in your God and
Be patient,
It will come to you sooner than you think.

The greatest feeling I had was meeting Les Brown on Mother's Day. It was exciting and I will never forget it. My success is my passion and I know God will help me make my dream come true. I want to empower women with self-esteem and self-confidence. I want to take this to the next level in life. Success lies in your hands and you need to tell yourself every day what you want to tell the Universe. You also need to keep praying and telling God what you want in life and believe in yourself always.

Stacey King is a single mother of eight amazing children. She always had a passion for becoming something great—an author—with the help of her God, her faith, and always thinking positively and believing in herself. Her dream came true: she is an author, co-author, and a speaker too.

Keep Your Head Up

by Stacy Boreland

It is very common to hear the line "never give up" from people. As a matter of fact, that line of advice is so common that it often means nothing these days. However, I am saying the same thing to you because I'm an individual who had excuses to fail in life, yet I still thrive.

It was always fascinating to watch the planes in the sky as I dreamt of having the opportunity to travel in an aircraft one day. The opportunity came when I was fourteen years old, as my dad got married and we migrated to Canada. I knew this was the best option for me because my mother had died when I was four years old, and my grandmother who had been caring for me died shortly before I migrated.

I started high school trying to fit in with the others as well as their styles, but instead, I was called a "freshie." I didn't know what it was like at that time to wear the best clothing or name brands, but I was grateful; my stepmom was doing the best she could. My style of dressing didn't stop me from learning and getting exceptional grades. Unfortunately, in the blink of an eye, things changed for the worse. We lived in a place known as Connections at Jane and Finch (the projects, government housing) in Toronto, and when I came home from school one day an eviction notice was on our door.

With nowhere to turn, I started to bounce from place to place until my dad was able to care for me on his own. I became pregnant at sixteen and was rejected by social assistance, I think because someone said I'd have to wait until my child was born. Nonetheless, I continued school and made honour roll every semester until I graduated. Today, I am a nurse by profession. I am also a home owner, proud mother of two university students, and a proud grandmother. And, I'm in the process of having my own clothing line. As I say, never give up.

Stacy Ann Boreland is a registered practical nurse and an upcoming entrepreneur in the process of having her own clothing line. Stacy has a strong faith in God and continuously encourages others to have faith, hope, and trust in God in whatever situation they're facing, and to pray without ceasing.

Facebook: https://www.facebook.com/profile.php?id=1606710332

Instagram: https://www.instagram.com/stacyboreland/

A Broken Arm

Stephen McDermott

Do you know why you are reading this? What brought you to this chapter, to this place, to this literary moment? Well, there exists a hidden ability within each of us to affect others. I can show you, but first I must summarize it in one sentence: You're reading this because my mom broke her arm.

In Dublin, Ireland in the mid-1950s, people had routines that you have now: wake up, eat, go to work, laugh, etc. Sound familiar? Not very interesting, right? Wrong. On one of those days, my mother, Pauline, broke her arm biking to work. Pauline probably didn't realize how she would influence the lives of people (including you). She was just going about her boring, everyday routine but this injury would have many wonderful consequences.

While Pauline recovered from her broken arm, her sister, Marie took over her job and met a good-looking bloke named Joe Carolan. Love flourished and Joe and Marie became engaged, got married and moved to Toronto to start a new life. Many years passed and Pauline with her husband Christy, eventually moved to Toronto to live close to Marie and Joe.

So kindly allow me to explain how these words arrived to you dear reader. You see, I became friends with Randi Goodman and wrote this piece for her. I wouldn't have written it if I hadn't met Randi, I couldn't have met Randi if my family hadn't moved to Canada, and remember, my parents chose Canada to be with Marie and Joe, but Marie and Joe wouldn't have met if Pauline hadn't broken her arm.

My point dear reader is to help you realize that you are extraordinarily important. Events have occurred and will occur in your life and you are making decisions right now that will impact other people; people that you may never meet. You are reading something empowering and inspiring because long ago, a lady that you probably will never meet, broke her arm. So dear reader, now that you are aware of this power, what will you do?

Stephen McDermott is a full-time, award-winning REALTOR® and a part-time trader on the S&P E-mini index. Born in Dublin, Ireland, Stephen grew up just outside of Toronto. His strong family values shine through every aspect of his life. A true optimist, Stephen enjoys helping others improve their lives.

www.stephenmcdermott.ca

Out of the Darkness

by Sulekha Patel

There she stood. At the edge of the cliff. Looking sunken, broken. Complete contrast to the beautiful colorful sky as the sun was setting against the endless ocean. Feeling the darkness inside, she raised her head and outstretched her arms, surrendering to what she had become. A strange feeling formed deep within her. She felt she would burst. She closed her eyes, afraid of the manifestation of her ugliness. What does pain, guilt, self-loathing look like? Would she be able to bear the truth?

From the centre of her chest burst a light so bright she fell back. Just as the sun set, from the blinding light emerged a white beautiful horse. It stood in front of her, radiating with beauty. She sat in front of this beautiful horse in disbelief. How could something so beautiful be for her? Yet, she felt at peace. She raised her hand, expecting the horse to recoil. Instead it came forward. She moved her hand back. She was not worthy of such a majestic creature. The horse moved closer, forcing her to rise. She raised her hand and touched its head. Like a soft stream of energy, the horse absorbed her darkness. She panicked, who would she be without the pain? A calmness was growing inside her and unconditional love surrounded her body.

She looked up and saw a more magnificent sight. A stunning unicorn glowing in pure light. She burst with love! As the horse came closer she saw her reflection in its eyes. She was shocked. The face that she saw was smiling. She hugged the unicorn and cried like never before. She let go of the pain and memories that hardened her. She felt free. Suddenly she was riding the unicorn across the sky. She felt so connected to life. She whispered to the unicorn to never leave her. In her thoughts the unicorn told her to close her eyes. It said they were always one. It was she who left.

When she opened her eyes, there she stood. At the edge of the cliff. Looking happy, strong and whole.

 Reiki master and crystal healing practitioner, Sulekha Joshi-Patel's passion for the human experience, started with her degree in psychology. As a senior HR professional, she was drawn to learn more about the art and science of energy healing. Now her mission is to share Reiki and spiritual healing with others.

Contact: sulekhapatel@bell.net

Imagine. Build. Play.

by Sumita Mukherjee

"Mommy! Mommy— look!" she yelled. Drawn by the sound of my seven-year-old daughter's giggles, I peeped, smiling at her delight with the fizzy mixture bubbling from the test tube. She was engrossed in her science play. My mind raced back to my own childhood; my grandfather and me tinkering in his under the staircase workshop, building balance beams, telescopes and heaps of other gadgets.

It wasn't always like this. After years of working in human resources, I arrived at my office one morning, my head exploding as a voice shrieked deep inside, "Is this for me?" My heart ached for the joy of exploring my own path. "Take a leap of faith," the voice whispered seductively.

That was it. I started by creating a series of travel adventure books for kids and found a publisher who believed in my dreams. Despite my overwhelming nervousness about leaving a stable career to take this step into the unknown, my first book sold over four thousand copies in Malaysia and Singapore. Kids were hungry for learning and WIZKIDS CLUB was born.

A science club for children aged four to fourteen, WIZKIDS encourages children to imagine, build and play. With the help of online videos, books, and toys, children are caught up in the experiments, barely noticing they are learning. A perfect combination of learning through play.

As I became caught up in my writing work, I realised that my daughter's playtime was spent glued to tablets. "This is no good, use your NASA STEM (science, technology, engineering, and maths) leader degree to create meaningful books," was my own call to action.

I created books with DIYs and activities for kids. WIZKIDS CLUB teaches science and engineering principles, giving children an educational head start. It's such a relief to see my daughter spend her time in creative play. This fulfilling experience is something all parents should invest in. Creating stimulating learning/play environments at home for kids from an early age can build 21st century leaders. My responsibility is to continue to inspire and keep tinkering on. I am Sumita Mukherjee, and I've taken the leap.

Sumita Mukherjee is a NASA STEM certified leader and children's book author. She founded WizKidsClub.com to raise the next generation of creative leaders. With engaging kids' activities, educational books, experiments, hands-on projects, DIYs, travel stories, and engineering books WizKidsClub is perfect for children from four to twelve years old.

www.wizkidsclub.com

Happiness From Within

by Suzette DaCamara

Wow! How time flies. Before you know it, you get to a certain age and it is like, how did I get here so fast? Things happen in our lives to teach us that we are only here for a period of time and we have no idea when our time is up. Things happen in our lives to teach us that we need to love one another, forgive one another, and compromise with one another sometimes in order to live in peace. Occasionally when you compromise it is not something you want to do, but you feel like it is necessary or perhaps even a must.

My whole life I've felt like I had to compromise at the expense of making myself happy. I am always doing things, everything as a matter of fact, to make others happy. But what about my own happiness? Do I not deserve to be happy? What is happiness? Why am I putting everyone's happiness before my own? Time is just ticking by, and before you realize it you reach fifty years old and you think, what the heck? When is it my time to deserve happiness?

There comes a time when you need to step back and analyze what is important in life. You need to pick and choose your battles. Every single breath that we take is important. Every single breath we take is a gift that we cannot, we must not take for granted. We must give thanks and praise for all the gifts, talents, abilities, opportunities, non-opportunities, accidents, mistakes, errors, and life lessons that we have every day of our lives.

You may feel like you are going through a rough period in your life, but you must look around and you will see that there are worse times and worse situations other people are facing every single day and that yours are nothing compared to theirs.

Every day we must wake up with grateful hearts, smiles on our faces, and the knowledge that with a positive mind and attitude, all things are possible including happiness in our lives.

Founder, CEO, Suzette DaCamara, Soul2Soul Healing, and Wellness, is a registered reflexologist; acupuncture detoxification specialist; first and second degree Reiki; program certified in professional counselling skills, and addictions studies and intervention strategies; with applied suicide and intervention skills training (ASIST). Suzette also has over twenty-five years' in accounting and finance.

Website: https://soul2soulhealing.ca/

Website: http://partnerscounselling.com/?page_id=1007

Facebook: https://www.facebook.com/ HolisticPractitionerSuzieDaCamara/

F.E.A.R.

by Tara Ellis

Transitions in life are supposed to be joyous. I think back fondly on some big moments in my life that were filled with undiluted joy. Unfortunately, those are not the ones that stick out in my mind.

I was born with several medical conditions. Before I even entered the world, the doctors told my mom I would not survive, would never walk, talk, think, or be able to function on my own. They even recommended that my devoutly Roman Catholic mom have an abortion or have me institutionalized!

That's what they said.

My mom and dad refused, took me home and raised me to thrive. I was told that being learning disabled I would not be able to handle university.

That's what they said, and they shredded my university applications.

Fast forward over thirty years, and over twenty-five surgeries and near-death experiences. I had my master's in social work, but I was struck by the most unmerciful pain imaginable. I was later diagnosed with a neurological condition, and was sent for months of testing, surgery, rehabilitation and no relief. I was told that my condition was incurable, and I was doomed to live my life in constant pain.

That's what they said.

I now realize that what they said was based on F.E.A.R.: False Evidence Appearing Real.

Their backgrounds and training created false paradigms of disability. The unequal power dynamics could have easily had me believe what I was told and behave or live accordingly.

That is not the choice I made, and it is not the choice I hope you make either. Someone's opinion of you does not dictate your reality, and no one can predict the possibilities the future holds.

Every person is here with a unique purpose and gift. You must seek your unique gift and share it with the world, because we need you.

If you choose F.E.A.R., let it be in this way: Face Everything And Rise.

Let nothing hold you back from being the best version of you. And to all the people who say you can't, answer this way:

Yes. I. Can.

Tara Ellis, disability empowerment strategist, and thought reformer has helped hundreds of youth and elderly overcome challenges over the last twenty years. The author of VisAble and Empowered, and creator of the VisAble and Empowered 10-Week Coaching Program, Tara has overcome childhood disability and mental illness struggles, and Chiari malformation.

Thank You for Letting Me Go

by Terry Holdershaw

Throughout the first seven years of operating my business, I supplemented my income with freelance work in the same field, and part-time jobs. For the last two years of those seven I took a full-time position with a competing business in the same event production and entertainment business I was in. This move brought a drastic halt to my business as I was focused on this position and had to limit my personal business offerings, but it gave me regular and steady work.

I spent two years helping to grow this business and someone else's dream. I gained a ton of experience, learned a lot, and started to become known within our industry while in this position. Near the end of this business relationship, the owner and I had some differences of opinion, and I was given the option to be fired or to voluntarily leave my position. This change was very abrupt and unexpected. At the time I had just moved into a new apartment with my girlfriend and had recently begun what would turn out to be a three-year divorce.

At first, I was scared and worried about what I would do and how I was going to pay my bills. In the events industry it's common for clients to hire suppliers six to twelve months in advance of their events. Even getting one new client could mean it would be a year until the work happened and I got paid. But, it didn't take me long to figure out this was one of the best things that could ever have happened. I made it an opportunity and a challenge to focus on my business full time. The experience also gave me the drive to do whatever I could to grow my business. Ever since then, my business has grown year after year. I'm now happily married to my wife who works in my business full time and I've never looked back.

Terry Holdershaw grew up in rural Nova Scotia. He moved to Toronto after high school, where he completed an audio engineering technology program. In college, he started his business, Scotia Entertainment Services which later changed names to Scotia Events Inc. Scotia provides audiovisual production services, DJs, and live entertainment.

www.scotiaevents.com

www.terryholdershaw.com

Rising Through Difficulties

by Teresa Hunt

As humans we are bound to experience changing times and situations in our lives. At some points we groove on seemingly pleasant moments while at others life presents itself as a spate of nightmares. Difficult times make us anxious. In fact, they are capable of stalling our plans and impeding our progress as we journey through life. For most people, coming back stronger out of these situations is a herculean task.

Having experienced this at one point or another in my life, I can boldly say that there is no magic formula that works for everyone.

It is determination, dedication and devotion.

Once a divorced mom of two, I managed to obtain three diplomas. Eventually, I became a paralegal. Life was not going according to my blueprint, but I still had immense belief and unwavering faith that things would get better. Then, just as I began to garner unbeatable confidence, the worst happened: I was diagnosed with histiocytosis. I became weary in body and soul, but I kept pressing forward, moving slowly yet strongly. I maximized my inner strength and fought through supremely difficult times, and against all odds.

This singular event would further open me to an avalanche of opportunities. I was already of the firm conviction that if I could literally defeat illness, nothing else was impossible.

I am now the president of a nonprofit, Histiocytosis Association of Canada, and a productive business called UR Bath Products that produces and sells hand-curated natural products. I also became the co-owner of Ontario Boat Wreckers, a renowned source for new and used boat parts, and to crown it all, I created To Your Defence Paralegal Services. In short, those hard, grueling times brought me down, but they were also the same forces that propelled me to call on my inner strength, and to achieve my dreams.

Like me, you can also rise above your difficult moments today with sheer determination, unparalleled dedication, and thorough devotion. All you need to do is to be confident, committed and courageous.

Teresa Hunt is a professional paralegal who has found her purpose in life. She has overcome obstacles and is now living a life of passion. Teresa is hoping to use her attained skills to give back to her community and assist people through legal matters and difficult times.

www.toyourdefence.com

Redesigning My Life

by Thea Cosma

Fifteen years ago, November 30, was a very significant day for me—a time of endings and a time of beginnings. In order to allow change and transformation, I needed to let go of the old so I could redesign my life. I was longing for a change. I wanted to see more of my children and my family, have time for myself, and find my passion. My body and my instincts were telling me that I was in the wrong job and on the wrong path, so after years of contemplation I left my job in the corporate world.

My new journey of growth and awareness was directing me to places I never imagined, synchronicities started to happen, and I was ready and open for something greater. My creativity was emerging too: I took painting classes at a local library, and studied interior design, one of my passions. Later, I met a feng shui teacher and studied with her. I was also led to a yoga studio where I was introduced to meditation, affirmations, and inspirational teachers; I took qi gong classes with a wonderful master who took me to the next level in my journey; and, I found myself reading motivational and self-improvement books and worked on my inner self for the first time.

As a result, some people in my circle began to disappear, which was a blessing, and my new mantra became, "I am surrounded by positive people." As I began to trust and let go of what was not working for me, my life was being redesigned. I started my own business as a feng shui and design consultant; joined design associations, and networking and spiritual groups; and I met and collaborated with other designers and feng shui practitioners on different projects. Eventually I started writing articles for various publications, which I loved.

Determination and most of all, belief and faith can shift our perspectives, and that is when we can redesign our lives any way we choose. It is important to trust your journey along the way—the universe is full of infinite possibilities!

Thea Cosma has specialized in and taught feng shui (the ancient art of placement), interior décor and home staging for the last fifteen years. Creating change, beauty, harmony, balance and positive flow of energy in spaces has been her passion. She also teaches feng shui certification classes.

www.theacosmainteriors.com

It is Not Over Till I Win

by Tonya Nelson

"It is not over until I win."
-- Les Brown

These are the seven words I live by every day, especially when I am going through down times in my life. I repeat these words in my mind until I manifest and believe that change is coming. In life we have to deal with two main phases in our journey: up times when life flows beautifully, and down times when life get extremely tough and unbearable. It is how we react to the down times that really shape who we are as women.

I learn more about myself as a woman during the down times than during the times when life flows beautifully. In up times you are so happy you truly believe it won't end, but it does at some point. It was January when I met him. He was handsome, sexy, with a beautiful smile and beautiful eyes, and milk chocolate skin. When I tell you I fell hard, I fell hard. This guy had everything I needed, and I envisioned spending the rest of my life with him. A few short months later I was sitting on my bathroom floor, tears streaming down my face, wondering to myself what was I going to do next.

Something beautiful came out of my heartbreak: I learned how to breathe. I learned how to meditate and grow deeper into myself. I learned to give to myself what I kept giving away to others. I learned to be grateful with the life I built. Whether it be financial hardships, loneliness, singleness, divorce, struggling to understand where to turn, what happens next, where to run, when to cry, whether to give up, or when to give in; you are not alone! Cry if you have to, scream, find someone to talk to, meditate, and most of all, confide in others and in a higher being.

Anytime you are in one of those down phases repeat these words to yourself over and over again:

I am my rescue.
I am enough.
I am a Queen.
I will rise again.

Sending love and light!

Tonya Nelson is an author with a dream of mentoring women to be something even greater and more powerful than they could ever imagine. She is passionate about relationship coaching and is in the process of writing her own book, Living My Worst Nightmare and Loving It.

LinkedIn: https://www.linkedin.com/in/tonya-nelson-a28b29109/

Contact: tonya.nelson9931@hotmail.com

The Call

by Tracy Hodge

The steam rose as I lay in the hot, salty water. It was September 9, 2012, a date that will be etched in my mind forever.

My husband answered the phone and somberly handed it to me. The horrible reality that I had breast cancer was confirmed when I heard my doctor's voice that fateful Sunday evening. She was as shocked as I was because the doctors had been sure that it was a cyst until the biopsy. Over the next several days, I went through a series of emotions ranging from disbelief, to anger, to finally settling into the acceptance that my choices in young adulthood had created this malfunction in my body.

After the surgery, scans confirmed that there were no other masses, that the three lymph nodes they took were clear, and that they had successfully removed the tumour. Through research, I discovered that the form of breast cancer I had didn't usually spread, despite being very aggressive. I also learned that the standard treatments would only decrease the chances of the cancer returning by ten percent.

My loved ones wanted me to have conventional treatments and the surgeon wanted me to at least have radiation. However, my decision that natural treatments were the right path for me was so clear and it made managing their emotions and fears much easier.

This was the beginning of the personal growth journey that I embarked on and still pursue today. I have grown as a person and have learned how to stand my ground in a firm and gentle way when presented with pressure from others. I am forever grateful to that cancer because, before it, I was dead; I just hadn't officially declared it. I was miserable in my life, unclear why I was here, and I disliked myself and my job. Today, I am a totally different person than I was then.

It is my hope that this story gives you the conviction to make choices that are right for you and gives you the courage and the strength to stand strong in those decisions!

 Tracy Hodge is an ISSA-certified personal trainer who specializes in Mom Mess to Goddess transformations in her business, Paths for Healing. Tracy is also a motivational speaker and a bodybuilder who participates in fitness competitions and was featured in the 2018 UFE Fitness Calendar. Tracy lives near Kingston, Ontario.

www.tracyhodge.com

Angel

by Vanessa Taylor

My friend you are, my lover I'd hope that you would be ... so, so intrigued by your presence,

hypnotized by your smile. I was afraid of the sneak peek into my future ... I somehow knew it

would be you. The sparkle in your eyes when we met, then .... the look of desire for something

that was forbidden. You understood that I was in a dark place, but your loving spirit knew that light and darkness could not exist in the same room and our spirits embraced ... you touched me. I believe in angels and God said you never know when you're entertaining one ... not knowing at the time that I was entertaining you in my thoughts! Always a word of encouragement, a smile in your voice, care and compassion. You became my reality in a world where true love fades like the morning dew.

I saw you in the corner of my mind, I was so deep in thought ... Do I tell the world that there is

someone new in my life, and there is ... would they respect me, respect my wishes?

I finally found the courage to try and move on, give someone else the opportunity to love me

and hope he will. Can he love me, unconditionally as I'm willing to do for him ...?

I found the strength with every fiber of my soul to say to someone new that I love him.

Vanessa Taylor is a pre-school, special education teacher in Stone Mountain, Georgia. She is a mother, grandmother, and published author of children's books. Vanessa enjoys life and loves God and writing for children to bring their fantasies to life and smiles to their little faces.

https://www.facebook.com/navymom2006

https://www.facebook.com/taylorgirl1999

Making Lives Better, One Life at a Time

by Vicky McGrath

My mom died from Alzheimer's in 2012, when she was seventy-four years old. Following my mom's death, I tried to comfort my dad as he transitioned to living life without my mom and on his own for the first time in over fifty years. I also thought about how we could have done things differently. What did a better outcome look like? What care options were available for my mom and the thousands of others at home, in the hospital or in long-term care with Alzheimer's? What support might we have provided to help my dad? What was going to happen as the baby boomers aged and faced illness and death in a healthcare system that was already in deep trouble?

It was about two years later that I saw part of the answer to my question. A small pink car was parked on our street: Nurse Next Door Home Care Services. Home care services? The company sent caregivers to your own home to help you during sickness, injury and old age. Who knew? And so, here I am today, the owner of a Nurse Next Door Home Care Services franchise, contributing to the solution by providing assisted living to people in their own homes.

Now, as I help people caring for loved ones with Alzheimer's I can honestly say, don't move your loved one! No matter how annoying or frustrating they are becoming, bring in as much help as you need to survive the phase. Every challenge is a phase: rummaging, wandering, agitation, aggression, refusing personal care, and mobility loss. It can all be managed at home, and you can arrange for assisted living in your own home when the primary caregiver is no longer capable of managing. As Dorothy said in *The Wizard of Oz*, "there's no place like home," wherever home may be.

Vicky McGrath is the co-owner of a Nurse Next Door Home Care Services franchise. Nurse Next Door was established in 2001, in Vancouver BC and has over 130 franchise locations across North America.

www.nursenextdoor.com

#Take5 Empowering Steps:
Five minutes, five times a day, for greater focus on your goals.

by Wendy Baird

Before you get out of bed #take5 minutes for yourself. You can spend this time doing any number of things, but the goal is to start your day refreshed. For me, I will often just lie there with my eyes closed and a big goofy grin on my face, not opening my eyes until I can feel the smile. Try it for just a moment. Close your eyes gently and smile big!

After your morning routine (everything you need to get done before you begin your daily tasks) #take5 minutes to listen to upbeat music or motivational speakers. Getting your mind set to just the right mood will allow you to accomplish more than if you are dragging yourself to work already looking for the day to be over.

If you are like I used to be during the time after lunch but before you are done with your work day—dragging, looking at the clock, and waiting to go home—stop what you are doing and #take5 minutes to listen to upbeat music or motivational speakers again.

Your day is done! At least your work day. Finish your daily routine, take time to enjoy dinner, and accomplish everything you need to in order to relax and breathe somewhere quiet, where you won't be interrupted. Now is the time to #take5 minutes and reflect on your blessings. Try writing down five things you are grateful for.

While you are feeling grateful and have let go of any stress you felt throughout the day, this is the time to #take5 and write down five goals for yourself for the following day. This could be things to remember, people to contact, or anything you have been putting off. Limit yourself to five items so you will feel accomplished after completing the tasks instead of feeling defeated by not checking off an entire list.

Be your own hero—#take5 and seize the day!

Wendy Baird has been through so much and now dedicates her life to helping others.

Her drive and passion are apparent in how hard she tackles and hits her goals. However, it's her ability to inspire and encourage others that people admire most about her.

Website: www.WendyBaird.com

Facebook: https://www.facebook.com/TheEmotionalEntrepreneur

Living in the Shadows

by Wendy Baird

Hi, my name is Wendy and I have been suffering from depression for almost fifteen years. What began as part-time sadness became crippling over the years. Many situations contribute to the overwhelming emptiness I feel within. I wish I could pin point just one or two, so I can begin to heal at a quicker rate, but the damage has been done and I must look towards a brighter future in order to begin to smile and move out of the shadow I call my life.

Those who have known me for years remember how negative I once was and are genuinely surprised at the changes I have made the last few years. I still feel all the pain, but I have found ways to cope with the continuing sadness. You see, I have been emotionally and physically abused so many times that I never found value in myself. I believed I did not and could not amount to anything in my life. I felt like a constant disappointment to those I loved.

It was not until I started helping others that I realized that I did in fact have a calling. That calling is to help others not feel alone. By offering a kind ear or a smile I have found that I can and do make a difference, not only in their lives but in mine as well. I stopped beating myself up over every bad situation and I started chalking it up to something I had to overcome, to become who I am today.

I am strong, powerful, and have a beautiful soul ready to be shown to the next person I meet. It's all right to let people into my life as long as I have boundaries. I can make a difference in this world one conversation at a time. All I need is to be aware of those around me and to trust my instincts.

I refuse to live in the shadows. I choose to share my heart with those open to hear my story. After all, every story has been written for a reason.

Wendy Baird has been through so much and now dedicates her life to helping others.

Her drive and passion are apparent in how hard she tackles and hits her goals. However, it's her ability to inspire and encourage others that people admire most about her.

Website: www.WendyBaird.com

Facebook: https://www.facebook.com/TheEmotionalEntrepreneur

Redefined

by Yomi Marcus

It's taken me a long time to get to this point. My past is full of days wondering where I fit in and why I couldn't measure up. I'd tell myself I wasn't good enough, pretty enough, capable enough, right enough. These thoughts made me feel small. Playing small quickly became my automatic response to living in this world. Small was safe. But it was also an unhappy and dark place for me.

The negative thoughts that controlled my life were constant: "Who do you think you are?" "Nobody wants to hear you." "You are pathetic!" "Just keep quiet!" So, I would retreat. For me, playing small meant taking minimal actions, anxiety and fear, holding back, and not speaking out or standing up for myself. It felt like being shackled to the ground while wanting so badly to soar.

Then one day, something shifted: I became aware of how these voices were affecting every aspect of my life. I asked myself the question: who would I be ten years from now if I continued my life with the same negative thoughts and definitions about myself? The answer hit me hard.

I realized, in that moment, that something had to change. I recognized that I had defined myself and my world with a negative and broken thought process. I could continue believing the lies that were keeping me small, miserable, and broken. Or, I could redefine myself and my world by allowing truth and light into my life. It was clear I had to redefine myself and reclaim my value.

To live life redefined is empowering. It means defining myself the way that only brings out the best version of me. It's a place where I can challenge the voices. I can let go of all the labels placed on me by others and those I gave to myself. I can choose what thoughts to live by today, and through that I can determine the person who I become ten years from now. I've noticed that the more I walk life redefined, the more open I am to amazing possibilities.

Yomi Marcus is a lifestyle coach who helps professionals create and define a lifestyle they love. She is passionate about supporting women, leaders, and groups as they release negativity, develop positive habits, and embrace who they are while nurturing a healthy mind, body, and community.

Website: www.herradcollective.com

Contact: hello@herradcollective.com

Instagram: https://www.instagram.com/herradcollective/

Planting Trees Through Transcendence

by Yulian Ihnatyuk

I remember this enticing walnut tree at my favourite cottage in Ukraine. One of my closest best friends, my loyal German shepherd, would wait for me while I challenged myself to climb it over and over. Conquering it felt amazing, yet my biggest satisfaction was the time spent on it: dreaming, looking to the sky and the stars as well as looking over the neighbourhood—not that the tree was that tall. My best friend certainly tried his best to join me, but it was out of his element. The gracefulness of the tree portrayed what it really meant to be at peace with oneself.

Learning about humans, such as Stalin and Hitler, was quite confusing. I was very surprised by the amount of hatred and sophisticated planning that was involved in killing millions of other humans as well as affecting many more. In university, as humbled participants of the March of Remembrance and Hope program, we faced the impact of such humans head-on. Clarity came through sharing our humanity. The biggest lesson is that the future should not be defined by the past. Whatever it is, as humans, we need to find our go-to tree before we can enter the future or we face the possibility of being lost.

What makes the world go 'round, what is exciting, and where does one fit in such a vast space? Learning about finance at university, and attending numerous events and lectures about Wall Street, as well as automation, energy, and artificial intelligence certainly piqued my curiosity. The tangible assets of real estate are amazing since they allow the possibility of creating sustainable communities that are smart and green, and that build for life. Most beautifully, this all can be done through mind-blowing designs that empower one's will for freedom. Passion can be powerful.

There is no bigger reward in life than seeing the sparks in people's eyes when they are not just happy but overwhelmed with consciousness. Hamlet once said, "To be, or not to be? That is the question…" Choose to be! I did, I do, and I will.

Yulian Ihnatyuk was born in the unique city of Lviv where culture and the mentality of East and West intersect. Entrepreneur, Ukrainian and community builder with a passion for real estate, finance and disruptive technologies such as AI, Yulian's mission is to leave a heartening and propitious legacy for humanity.

www.yuliani.ca

Conclusion

This book is a microcosm of life. Its short stories and poems represent virtually every type of challenge you could experience and overcome from leaving relationships, wrong careers, and war-torn countries; to overcoming abuse, drug and alcohol addiction, and mental illness; to healing after unexpected job loss or sickness; and finally, to surmounting issues that are far too common for many of us: fear and self-limiting beliefs; lack of direction and purpose; and a scarcity-based view of money.

But for all of that darkness, this book isn't dark; it's inspiring, because its stories s how how ordinary people who find themselves in extraordinary circumstances can triumph and become more than they ever thought they could. It's a book of transformation, and of healing.

Through their experiences, the authors learned how to stand up for themselves, love themselves, and believe in their own value. They learned how important it is to speak your truth; to seize opportunities and move forward even when you're afraid; and, to pursue the work that lights you up and allows you to make a difference in the world.

Most of the authors also learned that it's harder to write a short story than a long one, but they've done it, and we congratulate them! Less is more—much more—as their stories and poems prove. It is our hope that their insights, inspiration, and empowering spirit stay with you, and support you, long after you close the book.